HOW TO BECOME A BETTER TEACHER

Dale E. Griffin, General Editor
Oliver M. Schultz
Marian Baden
Ruth Hummel
Beverly Beckmann
Keith A. Loomans
Hal H. Whelply, Jr.
Donald A. Rosenberg
Les Schmidt

CONCORDIA®
PUBLISHING HOUSE
3558 SOUTH JEFFERSON AVENUE
SAINT LOUIS, MISSOURI 63118

ISBN 0-570-06364-7

Copyright © 1981 Concordia Publishing House
3558 S. Jefferson Avenue, St. Louis MO 63118

4 5 6 7 8 MP 96 95 94 93 92

Manufactured in the United States of America

Contents

Introduction

My observation has been that Sunday school teaching attracts some of the most gifted and consecrated people in the church. Volunteer teachers in the Sunday school possess a wide variety of Spirit-given talents, all of which enrich our Sunday schools. We can hardly ever be sufficiently grateful to the Holy Spirit for having endowed the church with so many gifted people who are willing to give of themselves and of their time to bring the Word of Life to God's people each week.

But even the most talented Sunday school teacher recognizes the need to grow not only in Biblical and doctrinal understanding, but also in the skills of teaching. The new teacher wants to know how to go about Sunday school teaching so he or she will be as effective as possible in sharing the treasure of the Gospel of Jesus Christ with others. The experienced teacher realizes the need to become even more proficient in the noble ministry of teaching the Word of God so that the seed of the Word brings forth much fruit. Even the professional teacher with years of experience recognizes the need to grow in order to avoid stagnation.

In this book eight experienced teachers of the Word share some of their knowledge and experience to assist volunteer teachers everywhere to develop their God-given talents and skills. Some of the material may be familiar, but much will be new.

Authors of the chapters in this book include Oliver M. Schultz, Marian Baden, Ruth Hummel, Beverly Beckmann,

Keith A. Loomans, Hal H. Whelply, Jr., Donald A. Rosenberg, and Les Schmidt. All are knowledgeable, dynamic teachers of the Word who have had many years of experience in the classroom. We thank God for these blessings to the church.

May the Spirit of God enrich you as you study these pages and apply to your own teaching ministry in the Sunday school the suggestions and insights of the authors.

Dale E. Griffin, Editor

Chapter 1

How to Prepare for Next Sunday

Oliver M. Schultz

Back in 1957 a national magazine dubbed Sunday school as "the most wasted hour of the week." The author did not intend to suggest that the Sunday school itself is worthless. He did say that too often Sunday school becomes worthless because the hour is filled with trivia; the hour is wasted because teachers prepare poorly or not at all.

If used wisely, much can be accomplished in that one hour of Sunday school. To get the most of that hour, determine in advance what you want to see happen to the students and plan all activities to help students attain those objectives. The day's lesson with its Scripture emphasis will form the core of the hour's session. To make maximum use of the Sunday school hour, plan all worship activities, select songs to sing, guide the lesson discussion, and provide learning activities that will lead students to the accomplishment of the goals for that Sunday's session. To do this requires careful planning.

Teachers can make the Sunday school hour more fruitful by planning an overall program for each quarter and for the year. One Sunday's activities should lead into the next. Planned coordination and integration of all sessions for the year can provide the students with cumulative growth in Christian faith and life.

WHERE TO BEGIN

As a Sunday school teacher you are the Holy Spirit's co-worker as He, through the Word you share, creates, sustains, and nourishes saving faith in you and in your students. Your ministry is to help students grow in their personal relationship with God through Jesus Christ. Your privilege is to lead students into greater maturity as Christian persons and to guide them as they learn how to think, feel, and behave as Christians in all areas of life.

You yourself can neither awaken faith nor strengthen it. This is the work of the Holy Spirit. But through the Word of God which you share with your students in Bible study, personal conversation, Christian songs, Scripture-based learning activities, and other ways, you are a person through whom the Holy Spirit awakens and nurtures the Christian faith and life of those whom you teach.

To be successful you need to be in tune with God. Through prayer you can constantly seek the Spirit's power, wisdom, and blessing in all phases of your ministry as a Sunday school teacher. Through your ongoing reading and study of the Scriptures, the Holy Spirit speaks to you and gives you the wisdom, understanding, and guidance that you need for your ministry as an ambassador for God.

As you prayerfully prepare your lessons, think of all the individual students in your group and of their needs. Remember them also in your prayers and ask God to use you to bring to them the Word they need.

GET YOUR BEARINGS

To plan an overall strategy for a quarter so your classes have reasonable sequence, at the beginning of a quarter skim through the lesson materials for that quarter. Discover for yourself how each lesson follows the previous one and how it leads into the next lesson. Identify the general theme and goals for the quarter.

Preparing a chart for the quarter can be helpful. At the top of the chart write the quarter's theme and goals. Then make a chart with thirteen lines (one for each Sunday) with six columns. Headings for the columns include: Date, Scripture Basis for the Lesson, Lesson Theme, Lesson Objectives or Goals, Relationship of Lesson Theme and Goals to Those for the Quarter, and Learning Activities.

Under "Learning Activities" you might include songs you want to sing (do allow for songs suggested by students), worship selections and activities, ways you will use to present the Bible narrative, learning activities to apply the Bible narrative, activities to reinforce main points of the lesson and its applications to your students, and memory work assignments. You also may want to provide for review of previous lessons at various points during the progress of the quarter.

You may want to use 13 manila envelopes large enough for collecting newspaper clippings and other learning resources. Use one envelope for each of the 13 Sundays in the quarter. On the front of the envelope write such pertinent information as the date of the lesson, the Scripture basis, the lesson theme, the lesson goals, and learning activities you have tentatively planned. As you come across ideas that may be helpful, write them down and place them in the appropriate envelopes. Newspaper and magazine clippings and other resources might likewise be placed in appropriate envelopes.

As the quarter progresses, ask yourself if you are using sufficient variety in resources and methods, if you are offering enough repetition to emphasize major points, and if you are providing for a logical sequence of learnings.

This kind of planning requires some time and effort,

but you will find the results well worth your preparation. You will find that each session will go more smoothly, that you and the students will have a sense of accomplishment as you progress smoothly from one lesson into the next, and that you will enjoy the exhilaration of confidence produced by being prepared.

FIRST THE FOUNDATION

Your ministry is to relate God, as He has disclosed Himself through the Scriptures, to yourself and to your students. The first step in your preparation of the weekly lesson is to immerse yourself in the Scripture basis for the next Sunday's lesson. As you study the Scripture basis, ask yourself what the text meant to the writer and to those who originally heard this Word of the Lord, what it means to you, and what it could mean for your students.

As you read the text, jot down on a sheet of paper important points of each verse and how they might be applied to yourself and to your students. Then, ascertain the central truth of the text which unifies the different points you have discovered.

Translations

To get still more out of the text and to experience the excitement of discovery, you will find certain Bible study tools very helpful. The Bible originally was written in Hebrew and Greek. You will likely be able to work only with a translation. No one translation captures all the shades of meaning and nuances to be found in the original text. But your understanding of the text can be enriched by comparing the translation you normally use with one or more of the many translations now to be obtained.

Most people prefer either the Revised Standard Version or the King James Version as their basic translation. For accuracy of translation we recommend the *New International Version* and the *New American Standard Bible.* Translations noted for their clarity are *The Holy Bible: An American Translation* by William F. Beck and the *Good News Bible: Today's English Version* produced by the American Bible Society. Two versions read widely with enjoyment are the *Living Bible* and J. B. Phillips' *The New Testament in Modern English.* These latter two versions are paraphrases rather than translations and need to be read with this caveat in mind.

Perhaps the best study Bible is the *New Chain-Reference Bible* (Indianapolis: B. B. Kirkbride Bible Co.) which can be purchased from your denominational publishing house or most Christian bookstores. This Bible uses the King James Version for the text and offers such study helps as a concordance, analyses of the Biblical books, maps, and a variety of other study helps. The *Amplified Bible* offers explanations of difficult words and concepts along with the Biblical text. The *New Oxford Annotated Bible with the Apocrypha* is a useful study Bible based on the Revised Standard Version. This Bible is especially useful for those who want access to the non-canonical Biblical books known as the Apocrypha.

Different translations in the classroom help the students as well as the leader to develop new concepts and ideas and to come to a definite conclusion related to the teachings of a given lesson.

As you read any translation it is important to note that the punctuation, paragraphing, chapter and verse divisions and headings, and similar helps are human additions to the text and are not part of the inspired Word of God.

If you in your preparation come across a particularly difficult passage, you will find help by consulting with your pastor.

Bible Dictionaries

A Bible dictionary offers information of places, people, and things mentioned in the Holy Scriptures. Even though you are able to visit such places as Jerusalem or Jericho today, you would find them substantially different from what they were in Biblical times. Therefore a Bible dictionary helps you to understand those places as they were in Biblical times.

A particular person or place may be mentioned a number of times in different circumstances in different books of the Bible. A Bible dictionary gathers these isolated bits of information together into one article to help you see the whole.

A Bible dictionary also offers historical information about persons, places, and things that can be helpful. For example, the ark of the covenant is foreign to our experiences today. A Bible dictionary will provide an account of its origin and significance as well as a description of its appearance. Wise use of a Bible dictionary can enable you to make the lesson come alive for your students.

Some study Bibles include a short dictionary.

Concordances

A concordance is an alphabetical list of important words used in the Bible. For each word listed the concordance lists the passages that use that word—as many as possible depending on the size and scope of the concordance used. You might use a concordance, for example, if you know that a key passage you wanted to find contains the word Savior. The concordance would list the passages using that word and enough words of the passage to help you locate the text you seek.

Concordances come in all shapes and sizes. Many concordances are found in the back of the Bible we purchase.

These are limited in their treatment of a word and cannot give you a very complete picture of a specific word or phrase.

In your lesson preparation you might use a concordance to learn how and in what contexts certain key words in the Bible basis for your lesson were used elsewhere in the Scriptures.

Cruden's Complete Concordance will prove adequate for your purposes. More complete concordances are *Young's Analytical Concordance, Strong's Exhaustive Concordance of the Bible,* and *Nelson's Complete Concordance of the Revised Standard Version.*

A topical Bible is somewhat similar to the concordance, except the topical Bible lists concepts or topics rather than words. For example, if your lesson deals with poverty, a topical Bible will list Bible references that deal with that subject. The standard topical Bible is *Nave's Topical Bible.*

Bible Atlases

Christianity is a historical religion. It is based on acts of God that occurred at specific times and places as well as on the Word He revealed to historical persons—prophets, evangelists, and apostles. To understand the Bible better, it is good not only to have some understanding of the historical background of Biblical narratives but also of the geography of Bible lands.

The standard Sunday school atlas is *The Westminster Historical Atlas to the Bible* edited by G. Ernest Wright and Floyd V. Filson (Philadelphia: Westminster, 1956). A more recent atlas that has gained wide acceptance is *The Macmillan Bible Atlas* by Yohanon Aharoni and Michael Avi-Yonah (New York: Macmillan, 1977). A third atlas many find helpful is *The Zondervan Pictorial Bible Atlas* edited by E. M. Blaiklock (Grand Rapids: Zondervan, 1969).

All three atlases describe the historical contexts of Biblical events in the light of geographical locations.

Bible Commentaries

In studying the Bible or in preparing for a lesson, it is well for you first to read the Bible selection and discover for yourself the message for you from that particular section. Then you may want to go to a commentary to discover what scholars have found in that passage. Thus you can check your discoveries with those of others, and you will find other insights you missed from your own reading.

A Bible commentary offers comments about the background of Biblical books and explanations concerning the meaning of the Biblical text. Not only will a good commentary help you understand Bible meanings better but it will also give you material for illustrations to help you apply the Bible lesson.

For your purposes a one-volume commentary is most practical. One of the most reliable and satisfying commentaries is the *Concordia Self-Study Commentary* by Walter R. Roehrs and Martin H. Franzmann (St. Louis: Concordia, 1979).

Should you desire more detailed information about a Bible selection, you might consult a multi-volume commentary suggested by your pastor or one in your church library. You will want to bear in mind that commentaries, especially extended ones, tend to reflect the author's views and do not possess the infallibility we associate with Scripture itself.

General Reading

Much *historical data* is difficult to accumulate and assimilate on the spur of the moment for the next Sunday's lesson. You will be better prepared if you include in your general reading the history of the ancient world as it pertains to the Bible. If you better understand the culture, environment, government, and what people believed and thought in the times in which a particular Bible book was written, you will better understand and be able to apply the message of that book.

For example, you can learn much about the culture in Abraham's time to help you understand better the Genesis narratives. Or, if you know something about the environment of the Arabian desert, you will understand better the hardships the children of Israel endured during the Exodus. The forms of government common in Bible times are quite different from those we enjoy today. Slavery was generally practiced and accepted. An understanding of this ancient institution will help you see how the attitudes and traditions of Israel were affected by slavery.

One of the best resources for understanding the historical background of the Old Testament is *A History of Israel* by John Bright (Philadelphia: Westminster Press, 1972). One good book on New Testament history is *New Testament Times* by Merrill C. Tenney (Grand Rapids: William B. Eerdmans, 1965). Another is *New Testament History* by F. F. Bruce (Garden City, New York: Doubleday, 1971). Your church or public library will likely have books on the historical background of the Bible.

Archaeology has uncovered much information about the high degree of civilization and culture of the ancient world. Through archaeological discoveries we now know much about the homes, the social structures, the science and technology, the arts and crafts, the economic structure, the languages, writing, and education, the religious beliefs and practices, and the literature and music of ancient peoples among whom Bible people lived.

Church history, especially that of the Lutheran church, will help you better understand your church today. For example, your study of the 15th and 16th centuries will help you understand why the Reformation was a necessity.

As a church school teacher in a Lutheran church, you need to know the doctrines of your church. A frequent review of the Small Catechism would be helpful. But as a teacher in the Lutheran church you would do well to become acquainted with all of the official doctrinal writings of the Lutheran church as we have them in the *Book of Concord* and to learn something about the historical circumstances that brought these writings into being.

In addition to reading, you can get a better understanding of Bible times by viewing artifacts from the ancient world. The Oriental Institute, Chicago, and the University Museum, Philadelphia, have rich holdings in artifacts from Bible lands. Other museums nearer your home may have some art objects that can help you better appreciate ancient cultures noted in the Bible.

RELATING THE LESSON TO YOUR STUDENTS

Having studied the Scripture text and the lesson notes for next Sunday's lesson, you now need to ask yourself how this applies to the students you teach. To do this you need to know your students.

You can learn much about general characteristics of students of the age level you teach by reading books and magazines. One particularly helpful series is the *Guides for Workers in the Sunday School.* This series, offered by Concordia Publishing House, Saint Louis, has a guide for every age level as well as one for church school administrators.

The most direct way to learn to know your students is to spend time with them and engage them in open conversation. Through conversation during the presession, in class, and in out-of-class settings you will learn to know their attitudes, skills, interests, and needs. You then will be better prepared to apply the Sunday's lesson to them where they are.

Home visitation is also important. Through home visits you will learn to know the home environment of your students and will better understand why they are as they are. Also, you can cultivate the active interest and cooperation of their parents so, together, you can help the students in their spiritual growth.

As you read the Scripture selection and lesson helps for next Sunday, reflect on how this applies to Jane or Jim. Perhaps you will want to make notes as you read. With your students in mind as you prepare, you will not only share information next Sunday; you will use the Scripture and lesson as means for the Holy Spirit to nurture the spiritual development of the people whom you teach.

MAKING A LESSON PLAN

Although your lesson helps offer a good outline for next Sunday's lesson, you will do well to develop your own lesson plan on the basis of your materials.

First, from your reading of the Scripture ask yourself "What is the point (central truth) of this narrative?" Then compare the point as you see it with that given in the lesson material. Decide on the central truth you will emphasize. Your lesson aims (desired outcomes), presentation, and activities all are to center on this one truth for the day.

Now consider how this central truth can be applied to your students with their individual needs and interests. For example, if your lesson is on Jesus' teaching His disciples to pray, reflect on the hurts and needs of your students. Consider how you can lead them to trust in God for His help and how you can help them in their prayer life. You may also want to teach them that God uses them to answer the prayers of others. Perhaps one of your students is insensitive to the concerns of his parents who pray for him. This may be an opportunity to help that student understand the pain he causes his parents and to be God's instrument for answering his parents' prayer.

Having mastered the central truth of the lesson, and how it applies to your students, write out in your own style the desired outcomes you hope to see accomplished in your students. Even though you use the outcomes suggested in the lesson book, writing them out in your own style will help you understand them better and use them more effectively. The entire lesson session with all its learning experiences and activities is to be directed to the accomplishments of these aims.

Desired outcomes are changes in the student you hope to see accomplished through study of a particular lesson. Changes include those in the students' understanding of the Bible and its meaning for them, in the students' attitudes and emotions, in their behavior, in their skills to live as Christian persons, and, above all, in their growth in faith in Christ.

If possible, word the outcomes in such a way that you can measure the results. This is not always possible because you cannot really measure the work of the Holy Spirit, but the attempt does help you be more pointed in your presentation. For example, your lesson may be that of Jesus teaching His disciples to pray. One desired outcome might be: That the student may be able to pray the Lord's Prayer from memory. You can measure this by asking the student to pray the Lord's Prayer from memory. Ability to do so will indicate to you that the student has achieved this particular desired outcome.

The central truth and desired outcomes will guide you as you prepare the remainder of your lesson plan. The next step will be to plan how you will introduce the lesson to capture the attention and interest of your students. You may wish to use the introduction offered in the students' guide, but you may want to get the point across in a different way. Or, you may use an entirely different approach, such as a recent event in your community that can be used to lead into the lesson.

Next plan activities for presenting the lesson proper. Activities might include the lesson in the guide, reading of the Scripture selection from the Bible, retelling the narrative in your own words, showing a film or filmstrip of the Bible narrative, or role-playing the lesson. Use of several different techniques in a session can increase interest and reinforce learning.

To reinforce the lesson and to measure student growth, provide review activities. The most common method is the use of questions and answers. Frame questions that will not only examine knowledge of lesson details but will also uncover student understanding of the lesson for everyday life. Hypothetical situations might be used to ascertain how the student might transfer learning of the lesson message to common occurrences and situations today.

The lesson plan might include suggested projects for students to follow to put the lesson into practice during the coming week. For example, if the lesson is on prayer, encourage students to pray regularly during the week. On the following Sunday you might ask students how regularly they prayed. Of course, this must be done in a way that will not embarrass anyone.

Worship activities should also be included at appropriate places in your lesson plan. Obvious places would be at the beginning and end of the session. But be flexible and allow for spontaneous worship during the session itself. Perhaps a student's need uncovered during the lesson discussion will lead you to pause to ask the class to pray for that student in his or her need.

ENRICHING THE LESSON

Your basic lesson plan will likely follow the material in the students guide rather closely. Through creative effort you can do much to make the lesson more personal for your class and to offer a greater variety of learning activities.

New Life in Christ curriculum materials include a teachers packet, and, for some grade levels, a student activity packet that contains flat visuals and student activities that can be used to add interest to the lesson and to reinforce the learning.

If you keep a file of illustrations you have clipped from magazines and newspapers, you can go to that file to find a clipping of a current event that illustrates the lesson.

Wise use of audiovisual aids can enhance the session. Filmstrips can be used to communicate the Bible narratives. Song records can be used to teach new songs. For example, if your lesson is on prayer, you might play a recording of a choral group singing an anthem or hymn on prayer.

CONCLUSION

Through wide reading, diligent study of Scripture, careful attention to the needs and interests of your students, and thorough preparation for every Sunday, you can make the Sunday school hour one of the most exciting and beneficial hours of the week for your students. This takes time but the results in the lives of the students you teach are well worth your efforts.

Chapter 2

How to Use the Presession Profitably

Marian Baden

IMPORTANCE OF THE PRESESSION

Sometimes Sunday school teachers view the presession as a time to be preoccupied with preliminary preparations. The presession can be defined as extending from that time when the students begin arriving until the formal worship, the class devotion, or, in some instances, the formal lesson, begins. For example, if Sunday school is scheduled to begin at 9:15, in all probability students will begin arriving around 9:00 and continue to arrive until 9:20 or so.

The presession is time often lost or wasted. To some extent, utilization of this time will depend upon where the students have been instructed to meet. In some cases the students will gather in the church or the fellowship hall for beginning worship before they ever go to their individual classrooms. In other instances the students will meet in their designated classrooms and either have opening devotions as a class or go as a class to the whole group worship.

During this time, from the moment that first child comes in the door, students will do *something*. It seems sensible, then, to plan for that time and structure it so that it doesn't deteriorate into a free-for-all. Allowing students some time to visit with each other does have merit, especially in circumstances where they don't see each other from Sunday to Sunday and need this fellowship. But when the presession time deteriorates into piano-pounding and black-board-scribbling time, it requires more planning.

Getting off to a good start can set the tone for the entire Sunday school sequence. Precious time can be wasted "settling kids down" after they have been unleashed into unstructured activity. Structured activity means more than a list of rules. The presession does require planning, but the planning can be well worth the effort. Before planning, stop for a moment to consider the function of the presession:

Function of the Presession

1. Getting acquainted
2. Merging individuals into a group
3. Completion of routine tasks
4. Motivation time
5. Getting set for the devotion/lesson

Sunday school classes are held in a wide variety of settings that range from a musty church basement room adjacent to the custodian's closet to a day-school classroom with all its vast array of distractions and untouchables. The time and energy most people spend arranging, maintaining, and attending to home and work settings show just how important environment is to human beings. Bright colors, orderly shelves, and posters on the wall make the learning task much more pleasant.

It is necessary to establish boundaries to protect those elements of the setting which do not belong to the Sunday school. Is a day school teacher's bulletin board being surreptitiously dismantled? Are those math games in the corner intended to be made available to the Sunday school class? Would the Ladies' Aid mind if their quilt blocks are lined up end to end on the floor to make a train? Each situation presents its own challenge.

MEETING THE STUDENTS

A preliminary contact with students and parents is often helpful. Home visits can be time consuming but also time well spent. Many parents have no idea who their child's Sunday school teacher is. Too many parents drop the children off at the door and pick them up in the same place. Too often Sunday school remains a mystical experience their children enter alone. Contact with parents of the children in the class can set the stage for willing volunteers to help with the program at a later date. Most of all, it will indicate that teachers care about the children in their class enough to come to visit. An effective Sunday school program needs the cooperation and Christian influence of parents.

Even if a home visit isn't possible, a letter to the parents can be helpful. The main purpose of such a letter is to make contact with students and their parents and to welcome them to the Sunday school. Warmth is the primary ingredient. Such a letter could include two elements:
1) What you as a teacher promise to do
2) What you as a teacher expect of the children
A letter to new pupils might look something like this:

Dear Sandy,

Welcome to our Sunday school class! We look forward to having you join us each Sunday from 9:15 until 10:00. Your mother and father are welcome to come and visit too. We are meeting in Mrs. Piper's classroom at the south end of the main hall. We hope you can be here at 9:15 sharp because we've planned some interesting things to do. We promise to be there waiting for you.

Your teacher,
Mrs. Meyer

The initial orientation often sets the stage for later sessions. Let the students know what is expected of them when they come into the room. Where are they to put their coats? Where are the drinking fountains and bathrooms? Where should their offerings be placed? Having a special container for offerings and keeping it in the same place each week helps establish this routine. An established routine makes children feel secure. A friendly, welcoming smile makes children feel at home.

Name tags can be helpful at certain grade levesl if students aren't already well acquainted with one another. Some monthly suggestions could be:

January—snowflake
February—heart
March—cross
April—butterfly
May—flower
June—shell
July—triangle
August—crown
September—leaf
October—scroll
November—cornucopia
December—star

When children arrive each Sunday, some may need help with their coats, boots, or mittens. It is helpful to plan the presession so that the teacher is free to attend to these needs instead of being preoccupied with last-minute preparations. If such preparations are necessary, perhaps the children can be involved in helping.

Checklist for Initial Orientation

______ place for coats
______ name tags
______ container for offerings
______ chart for recording attendance
______ plan for late-comers

Stragglers or late-comers can be a problem. If the class leaves to attend worship in another room, make sure the late-comers know where to go or what to do. A sign on the door, a note in a conspicuous place, or simply verbal instructions to "wait" can help these children know what they should do. Children who walk in during the middle of the lesson are another potential problem. Plan ahead for taking care of presession activities such as attendance record-keeping for late-comers.

When welcoming visitors or enrolling new students, make them feel like invited guests rather than intruders. Encourage the children in the class to share whenever materials won't go around.

Quite likely there will be a child who objects to being left by his parents in a strange room. This is particularly true on the preschool and kindergarten levels. Determine ahead of time what to do if this situation arises. Will you encourage the parents to sit in on the session or will you feel uncomfortable with adults watching your class? Will you take the child on your lap and attempt to make him feel more secure through such physical contact? Will you enlist the help of another child in the class in making the insecure child feel more at ease? Will you allow the child to go home and be happy to be relieved of the problem? Chances are there is no one sure solution appropriate to all circumstances. Tactics depend upon the individual child and the individual teacher. But planning ahead and anticipating this problem and thinking about some possible solutions can help when confronted with the situation.

MAKING THE BEST USE OF THE PRESESSION

The importance of being early has not been overrated. It is difficult to structure activity if you aren't on the scene. If the children arrive before the teacher, they will take command. Being on the scene and ready to go puts the teacher in charge. Children who are ill at ease in an unfamiliar setting should also be considered. A smiling face meeting one at the door can mean a great deal to a child who is fearful, shy, or hesitant. It helps the children to know that they can depend on the teacher to be there. Being early also allows time to check the condition of the room. Are the heat, lighting, and ventilation satisfactory? Can adjustments be made to make the room more comfortable?

Being early also enables one to check whether all equipment necessary for the session is in working order. Does the record player need an extension cord? Does the projector need a new bulb? Being early allows one to make a last-minute check to be sure all the materials necessary for the lesson have been gathered.

As the children arrive, a teacher has several options:

1) Have the children sit down at chairs and tables and expect them to wait quietly until class begins. One can dream, but this is hardly a realistic expectation. Children who enjoy waiting and will sit quietly while doing so are an endangered species.

2) Talk to them and keep them amused. This may work well if the children realize they are a captive audience and are resigned to listening. It can also be difficult to maintain

interesting commentary week after week without becoming redundant.

3) Let them move at will around the room. Movement such as this may not take the anticipated form of silent meandering. It may even be uncomfortable for the teacher and adjacent classes in form, volume, and speed. Children may even run—and/or yell.

4) Spend the presession time learning more about the students through informal conversation.

5) Use prepared interest centers. Interest centers are planned activities that can be correlated with unit themes. They can also be used to go over memory work or review previous learning. Imaginative use of the presession through interest centers offers many motivational possibilities as well.

Structuring the presession is not something to be taken for granted; it takes careful planning. The following are some suggestions for activities which could be used during the presession.

Publications such as *Happy Times* can be used to advantage during the presession. A book center display of a variety of Arch Books, for instance, can be a simple way to occupy the children profitably when they first enter the room. Various parents may be willing to stay when they bring their children and assist with story-reading for the Sunday school presession. For older children a display of books is probably sufficient. Maintaining a file of past issues of periodicals can be a fruitful resource for presession time in future years. The following is a chart of the various periodicals available.

Department	Years	Magazines
Nursery	Ages 2½—4½	*Happy Times*
Kindergarten	Ages 4—5	

Primary	Grades 1 & 2	*Story Times*
Junior	Grades 3 & 4	*My Devotions*
Preteen	Grades 5 & 6	*My Devotions*
Junior High	Grades 7 & 8	*My Devotions*

INTEREST CENTERS

Some Sunday school teachers set out a table of blocks, one of clay, or perhaps one of puzzles to keep younger children occupied during the presession time. It is a challenge, however, to plan Bible-related activities which also serve as a factual review or motivating device for the Sunday school. Bible story leaflet pictures may be mounted on a bulletin board and discussed as a review of past sessions. An appreciation center utilizing pussy willows, a cocoon, or an assortment of shells or fall leaves can be gathered to point to the beauty of God's handiwork. Another suggestion would be to list Bible references on different portions of a Bible story picture. When the passage has been looked up and read, that part of the picture may be colored. Interest centers require some preparation. Parents and students can be asked to assist in the bringing or making of things for the centers.

MEMORY WORK ACTIVITIES

Memory work is often one of the more routine aspects of Sunday school. To add variety to the practice of learning Bible verses, activities can be developed which give the students additional practice in memorizing Scripture. One such activity can be called "Scrambled Eggs." A Bible verse is printed on a strip and then cut into pieces, word by word. These words are then placed into a plastic egg. The task is to unscramble the Bible verse by arranging the words in the proper order.

Another memory work activity might proceed as follows. Two teams are selected. A leader reads the beginning of a Bible verse from a prepared list. Team members take turns attempting to complete each verse correctly. The team who correctly completes the most verses wins. This could also be developed into a version of "Bible Baseball" with a diamond drawn on the board. Each attempt to complete a verse by a player is either a strikeout or a hit. Only runs driven in count as a team score. Three strikeouts retire one team and give the other team a turn.

Finally, a memory work activity could be designed as a board game. The first few words of a verse would be printed on a card. Players draw a card from a face-down pile, advancing according to a throw of dice if they complete the passage correctly.

USE OF THE RECORD PLAYER AND TAPE RECORDER

Playing records or tapes can profitably occupy children as they arrive for Sunday school. Such activity requires a minimum of preparation on the part of the teacher. Each year the Concordia Vacation Bible School materials include song records. These and other records could be kept on file in a record library for later Sunday school use.

Suitable records and cassettes would include the following:

Plattertales (storybooks with records), by Dan Burow, ages 3—8, Concordia

The Purple Puzzle Tree Series, ages 3—10, Concordia

Arch Books Aloud (1 record plus 2 Arch books), ages 4—8, Concordia

Shout and Sing for Joy (songbook available), ages 3—8, Augsburg

Tell Them I'm a Child of God (songbook available), ages 9—youth, Augsburg
Have You Heard the Good News? (record or cassette), ages 3—12, Augsburg
He Lived the Good Life, by R. Wilson, Augsburg
We're All God's Children, ages 4—8, Augsburg
Tell Me a Story Cassettes (6 sets), Augsburg
Jesus Style Songs, Volumes I and II, Augsburg

PURPOSEFUL GAMES

There are innumerable games and activities, both commercial and teacher-made, which would be appropriate for use in the Sunday school presession. For example, crossword puzzles and "Scripture Crostics" afford a quick review of Biblical facts. "Storybooks" offer an opportunity to retell and review a familiar Bible story. Coloring books could be merely busywork or they can be used as motivation for review of Bible facts. Children may color a certain portion of their picture when they successfully answer a question reviewing the story depicted. This activity continues until all children have all portions of their pictures colored. The teacher can adjust the difficulty of the questions to the capability of individual children so all can feel success.

Fingerplays or hand actions which accompany simple verses or songs offer a good icebreaker and provide involvement for young children. Not many commercial games are available to reinforce religion lessons. "Jesus and the Fisherman" is one which can be purchased. Better still, a teacher's ingenuity can adapt numerous well-known games to review Bible stories. For example, checkers could be played on a checkerboard which has a review question written in each square. Some commercial games, puzzles, and coloring activities which can be used for review include the following:

Card Games

Scripture Cards, American Bible Society; Griggs Educational Service

Blank Playing Cards (for creating games), Griggs Educational Service

Instructional Cards for Student Creativity, Griggs Educational Service

I Tell About Jesus (photo story cards with questions), ages 4—8, Augsburg

Puzzles

Bible Crossword Puzzles, Griggs Educational Service

Picture Puzzles and Quizzes: Bible People, by M. Cathcart, Standard

Junior Bible Crossword Puzzles, Augsburg

Scripture Crostics, by R. Helle, Concordia

Child of God Puzzles, Concordia

Bible Puzzles (duplicating masters for Old and New Testaments), Augsburg

Coloring Activities

Dot-to-Dot Drawing and Coloring Books, Augsburg

ABC Easy-to-Color Pictures, Augsburg

Jesus and His Apostles (coloring book), Augsburg

Giant Mural Coloring Books (Garden of Eden, Noah's Ark, Good Samaritan, and the Joy of Easter), Concordia

Jesus Mural Coloring Cloth, Augsburg

Jesus Coloring Book Series, Augsburg

"Thank You, God" Coloring Books, Augsburg

Bible People Coloring Books, Augsburg

Fingerplays

Bible Teaching Finger Plays, by M. White, Concordia

Bible Fingerplays for Young Children, by P. Shely, Concordia
Finger Fun, (fingerplays and action games), Augsburg

Kits and Other Games

System I (kit for making games), Griggs Educational Service
Jesus and the Fisherman (Storybook and spinner game), Augsburg
Bible Times Village to Make, Augsburg
Coins of the Bible, Augsburg
Pick-O-Rama Kits (Stand-up figures for retelling Bible stories), Concordia
Cheerful Cherubs (Bible-centered activity books) Concordia

The presession can also be used to good advantage for ongoing projects which take several weeks to complete. Some suggestions would be banner-making, puppet-making, or mosaic or mural construction. Banners can be glued, sewn, or embroidered on felt, burlap, or other fabric backgrounds. They can be used to enhance and add color to the Sunday school room, created as gifts, or taken home as the students' own room decorations.

Puppets can be made from paper bags, felt, or even cardboard-backed coloring book figures on a stick. Finger puppets offer additional variety. These can be made using a felt, fingertip-sized cone for each. Tiny eyes can be purchased in a hobby shop, fringe can be used for hair—imagination can dictate the rest. Puppet-making is an intriguing presession activity, and the completed puppets offer innumerable options for Bible story dramatization, both during the presession and during the regular lesson. Older children and youth may enjoy making puppets to be used by younger Sunday school children. The following are some helpful idea books:

Banners

How to Create Banners, by V. Broderick and J. Bartholemew, Concordia
See His Banners Go, by J. Marxhausen, Concordia
Signs of Celebration, by E. Lauckner, Concordia

Puppets

Teaching Bible Stories More Effectively with Puppets, by R. Sylwester, Concordia
Shadow Puppetry for the Church School, Augsburg
Puppets with Pizazz, by J. Wilt, Concordia
More Puppets with Pizzazz, by J. Wilt, Concordia

Project Resource Books

77 Dynamic Ideas Book (series of six books), Concordia
30 Bible Story Projects to Make, by H. Gramelsbach, Concordia
Recycle Catalog II, by D. Benson, Concordia
Can Make and Do Series (four idea resource books for very young children), by J. Wilt, Concordia
Christmas Games and Crafts for Chidlren, by S. Beegle, Concordia
Creating and Playing Games with Students, by J. Schaupp, Griggs Educational Service
Creative Activities in Church Education, by P. Griggs, Griggs Educational Service
Family Evening Activity Devotions, by R. Brusius and M. Noettl, Concordia
Making Old Testament Toys, by M. Hutchings, Augsburg
Making New Testament Toys, by M. Hutchings, Augsburg
Kirigami, Concordia
Year 'Round Crafts for Children, by J. Mobly, Concordia
38 Recipes for Bulletin Boards and Art Projects That Christian Kids Can Make, by J. Staffeld, C. Bell, and J. Kemp, Concordia

Year 'Round Patterns Book, Augsburg
Kindergarten Patterns Book, Augsburg
Preschool Pattern Book, Augsburg
Bible Things to Make and Do from Boxes, by D. Thompson, Augsburg

Resources

Resources for the presession offered by various publishers constantly change. Some items are withdrawn and new items are introduced. For current resources available for your presession activities consult your latest publishing house catalog. Addresses of publishers represented in this chapter are:

Concordia Publishing House
3558 South Jefferson Avenue
Saint Louis, Missouri 63118

Augsburg Publishing House
426 South Fifth Street
Minneapolis, MN 55415

Griggs Educational Service
1731 Barcelona Street
Livermore, CA 94550

American Bible Society
1865 Broadway
New York, NY 10023

Chapter 3

How to Plan for Meaningful Sunday School Worship

Ruth Hummel

WORSHIP IN SUNDAY SCHOOL?

Worship in the Sunday school? Does it really belong there? Isn't the purpose of Sunday school to teach Bible lessons? Isn't worship best done in the regular church service with the gathered congregation of believers? Isn't church for worship and Sunday school learning?

Yet what is worship? Does it not include our expression of the worth of God for our lives? We learn of the worth of God through instruction in His Word to which we respond in praise and prayer. Actually instruction is an important part of the church service through which the Word of God is taught through the reading, exposition, and application of Scripture and through the administration of the visible means of grace—the sacraments of Holy Baptism and the Lord's Supper.

Likewise, in a sense all of Sunday school is worship. Some people have defined worship as being *sacramental,* the bestowal by the Spirit of God's gifts to human beings, and *sacrificial,* the offering of self to God through praise and prayer. These two worship elements are present also in Sunday school. Through the lesson the Holy Spirit offers students the grace of God in Jesus Christ through the Word of God that is taught. Through hymns, songs, and prayer students praise and thank God for the gifts of His grace.

In this chapter, however, the subject of worship is limited to the formal worship period conducted at some point during the Sunday school session. One advantage of the Sunday school worship exercise is that it offers students opportunity to worship on their specific level of maturity. In addition to the devotional aspect of Sunday school worship, this period, if planned carefully, can also fulfill numerous educational aims. Some of these are:

To enable students—

1. To learn the hymns and spiritual songs of the church;
2. To learn the meaning of the liturgies used in the church's services;
3. To learn to pray;
4. To become acquainted with sections of Scripture;
5. To learn spiritual truths as given in the catechism;
6. To learn acceptable church decorum and the meaning of the various physical actions used in worship;
7. To learn more about the church's missions;
8. To learn the significance of the offerings of people for the church's mission; and
9. To be reinforced in the lesson theme for the day through the hymns, prayers, and message chosen for the worship period.

MAKING WORSHIP MEANINGFUL

It is a truism that we learn best by doing. People of the TV generation tend to look on rather than to get involved. They especially need to *do* worship and not just learn *about* it. The Sunday school worship period needs to be true devotion and not merely the automatic following of a set routine. As our Savior indicated in John 4:24, sincerity is to characterize all worship.

What is Worship?

To worship with meaning, students need to learn what worship is: the courtesy or reverence paid to worth; hence, honor, respect, reverence, and adoration paid to God. When Christians come together and hear God's Word, they hear what God has done and is doing for them. This hearing is to create a sense of deep gratitude which naturally produces the "worth"-ship response of joy, praise, and dedication. That sense of awe and thankfulness is worship, whether it occurs in church, in Sunday school, at home, or at a picnic. Through worship sessions and at appropriate places in lesson presentations, students can be led to understand the nature of Christian worship and to appreciate the important place worship is to have in their lives.

Age-Level Focus

An important advantage of worship in the Sunday school is that worship experiences can be easily planned for the various levels of maturity of the students. Worship for the small child can include simple songs, activities that appeal to small children, and the use of a vocabulary limited to words and concepts young children easily understand.

Older children can begin to learn the more sedate hymns of the church and liturgies of the congregation. They can begin to use adult versions of the Bible. Some Sunday schools form a children's choir which sings not only in Sunday school but also in the formal worship services.

As people mature, their interests become more differentiated. To involve youth and adults in worship, Sunday school leaders can identify their tastes, interests, and abilities to guide them as they plan worship experiences for these people. Some youth may like Baroque music and play Baroque instruments. These people can be invited to contribute their interests and talents to the Sunday school worship. Others like more contemporary types of music of which worship leaders need to be aware.

To focus on maturity levels of the students, most Sunday school leaders plan departmental worship. Small Sunday schools usually worship in two departments—one for young children up through grade two, and the second for all students above grade two. Others have three departments—one for those in grade two and under, one for students in grades three through eight, and one for youth and adults. Very small Sunday schools have but one department for the entire Sunday school, and very large congregations may have a departmental worship for each grade level until the high school years.

If worship is to be meaningful for Sunday school students, you must know your students and then plan activities which they can readily understand and which appeal to their interests.

Student Participation

There is probably no better way to make worship meaningful to students than by giving them opportunities to participate in worship activities as much as possible. They must not be led to think of their role as only that of a listener, a watcher, a part of the audience. When the individual abilities of the students are known and kept in mind, devotions can be planned to encourage maximum participation. A good reader can read the Bible selection, a student who has composed a prayer can read it, and the hymn can be accompanied by a student who has learned to play some musical instrument.

A regular order of worship or regular use of certain elements in the devotions can lead to familiarity and expectancy—thus encouraging active participation. Some variety will prevent boredom and thus lack of participation.

Students should be expected to understand what is used in the devotions and why. New hymns may be introduced with a sketch of the background of the hymns. The use of questions can help the worship leader ascertain how well students understand what is being done in worship.

To maintain student interest and participation, the worship period should be kept quite brief.

It might be helpful for the worship leader to be aware that there seems to be three types of possible involvement—that of the body, of the mind, and of the heart. Little wigglers may most need the first kind, junior high youth a greater proportion of the second, and all of us lots of the third.

Physical involvement is possible with any age group. Little ones can bring up their offerings individually, clap the rhythm or do the motions of a song, or act out a simple Bible story. Older children can carry in the Bible, pass the offering plates, light the candles, or act out Bible narratives on a somewhat sophisticated level. High school youth might take field trips and engage in projects that require considerable physical activity.

Mental involvement concerns remembering, comparing, solving problems, deciding. Even small children can recall story details, choose between two songs, or decide which of two actions is right. Increase active listening by giving students something to listen for in a song or a prayer. Speaking is more involving than listening, so let them speak the words of prayer or a song after you.

Let children who can read paraphrase the words of a new song, read the prayer in unison, read the psalm antiphonally, or tell why a Bible character acted as he did. Rising for prayer involves students physically and offers opportunity to explain the meaning of this worship action.

Involving the emotions and feelings of worshipers is the most difficult kind of involvement to attain. Sincerity is essential to true worship, and this must begin with the worship leaders. They must not only be sincere, but be able to communicate their sincerity. All adult leaders in the Sunday school need to participate along with the children. Adults who huddle in a corner during the worship session to converse or to make last-minute preparations can defeat the whole purpose of the Sunday school worship session.

Leaders must start where their students' thoughts and emotions actually are—whether they are at a recent sports event or an approaching party. Include the longings of students in your petitions and their victories in your thanksgivings; this will demonstrate that feelings must be involved in our worship forms. Respecting and encouraging self-expression will help keep truth in worship.

Relate to the Lesson

Worship will be more meaningful if it is related to the central theme in the lessons for the day. Hymns, prayers, meditations, and other worship activities related to the lesson will help introduce the theme for the day, or, if the worship session concludes the Sunday school, will help reinforce the truth students have learned.

The worship leader can relate the worship period to the lesson in a variety of ways. For example, the leader can read, or arrange to have an older student read, the Scripture background for the lesson in a Bible version easily understood by Sunday school students. A person might present a visual meditation based on the lesson theme, such as use of a flannelgraph or an object talk. One reason for departmental worship is that it can be more easily related to the lesson than an assembly of the entire Sunday school.

PLANNING THE WORSHIP SESSION

The Leader

For some Sunday schools the superintendent automatically is worship leader. However, the talents necessary for being a good superintendent are not identical with those needed for the worship leader. Moreover, if worship sessions are conducted in departments, a worship leader is needed for each department. It is best for the superintendent to coordinate the worship sessions, but to select leaders who have the talents important for leading worship.

The pastor may wish to lead the worship in one of the departments, or he may wish to conduct the worship periodically in each of the departments. Serving as worship leader, at least occasionally, gives the pastor the opportunity to develop a pastoral relationship with students.

Possibly several worship leaders may be chosen for each department. One may serve as overall leader while others may serve according to their talents; for example, one person with marked musical abilities may serve as song leader.

Actually, all the Sunday school teachers are to be involved in the worship period. They, as well as the leader, serve as examples of worship decorum. They are to be completely involved in prayer and praise—and *not* in taking attendance, drinking coffee, straggling in late, or standing to one side observing the "children play church." Teachers can actively help students in such activities as finding worship resources in the hymnal or in going through the motions of an action song.

The special gifts of teachers can be utilized. A musically-talented teacher may teach new hymns or play the piano or another instrument. Other teachers may be willing to serve as worship leader for a month or a quarter. Periodic changes of worship leaders allow each leader to learn from others and give variety to the worship session.

Members of the congregation are an important resource. A finance board member might explain what happens to the offering each Sunday. An altar guild member might explain the meaning of symbols on the paraments. Other adults might tell what their Christianity means to them in everyday life. Use of members will add variety to the worship period and will help unite the congregation as members give and receive from one another.

The Worship Center

Most churches today have more than one facility for the worship session. Older students may meet in the church sanctuary while others meet in the church basement. An educational building may have large rooms so a worship period can be held in each room. If only one space is available, one group might worship at the beginning of the Sunday school period and the other at the end.

Whatever space is used, many things can be done to make it a center for focusing thoughts and hearts on the worship of God.

Some use an altar for a worship center Wherever this is done, the altar should be reserved only for worship purposes and not be used as a catch-all for assorted presession toys, books, and teachers' handbags. Students can learn to respect the altar as a symbol of the presence of God among His people and to take care of it.

The altar can hold candlesticks and flower vases filled with flowers; it can be covered in a color appropriate for the liturgical season. Where an altar is not used, a small table or lectern can be a focal point. Banners and pictures can be distributed about the room to enhance the atmosphere of worship.

Candles might be lit and extinguished by students in a reverent, dignified manner. Thus children and youth will gain experience for serving as acolytes in the congregational service.

Plan for Unity

So much can be accomplished in the worship session that a leader must select what she or he will do on a specific Sunday. The leader does well to select first a theme to provide a focus for the period.

This theme may be taken from the lesson for that Sunday. The Teachers Guides in the *New Life in Christ* Sunday school materials offer worship suggestions for each Sunday. Thus the worship will reinforce the day's lesson. Of course, the leader will want to be flexible and make changes to meet the situation in the specific Sunday school.

Some leaders prefer to use the church year as a guide. Use of the church year provides orderly progression and offers opportunity to prepare students to join in the congregational worship with better understanding.

As a worship leader, you may prefer to follow the lesson themes for most of the year, but take note of the church year on special days and major festivals.

Plan for Variety

For many Sunday schools worship is a routine activity in which the same pattern is followed Sunday after Sunday. Students soon become bored; teachers and leaders merely go through a rote routine without reflection.

The leader must plan ahead if the worship period is to offer an orderly progression and yet provide wholesome variety. The leader may plan ahead for a month, a quarter, or even an entire year.

First, identify the theme for each Sunday during the period being planned. Then choose songs and hymns for each of the Sundays. You might use the first stanza of a hymn each Sunday for a month to help students memorize that stanza. Plan a varied music program so you can use guitars and other instruments as well as the organ or piano.

If you have some kind of address, plan different approaches. One Sunday you may have an object lesson, on another a chalk talk, and on another a flannelgraph lesson. Select in advance people to give these talks.

Many Sunday schools have memory work as part of the worship period. For example, the Sunday school may say in unison the 23d Psalm for every Sunday for a month or so until students can recite the psalm from memory. Catechism and Bible selections can thus be taught in a pleasant fashion. But you need to plan your memory program in advance if it is to be truly meaningful.

However well you plan the worship session, be ready to make on-the-spot adjustments during the worship period. Perhaps the pianist must be excused at the last moment. You then will need to find a substitute or use a different medium such as a record player. Or, students may clamor to sing a favorite. The leader who is well-prepared is usually adept in making needed adaptations.

Worship Decorum

Children who attend church services know that they are supposed to sit quietly in church, stand at certain points in the service, and go through other actions. But they may not know why they are to behave thus. The Sunday school worship period is not only a good setting in which to teach students appropriate church manners, but also to teach them the significance of the various worship actions.

At least once each year it would be well for some person, perhaps the pastor, to give students a simple explanation of the service and of worship actions. During the year these actions, such as standing for prayer, may be followed in the Sunday school worship session.

Teaching New Songs

Each department of the Sunday school should have at least one leader capable of teaching new songs. There are many effective methods of teaching songs. One of the best, especially for young children, is to teach a new song by rote. The teacher asks the children to listen as she sings the song and then invites them to sing with her. Young children need to hear many repetitions of the song before they have learned it. Words and music are best taught together. Take time to explain the meaning of the words to the children. For some songs, pictures can be mounted on a chart to help little ones remember the words and their sequence.

Leaders who lack confidence in their musical ability, or who seek variety, may use records. Many good records are available (cf. chapter two). A recording can be played several times during the presession to help students become familiar with the song before it is taught formally; this will lessen the number of repetitions necessary for teaching the song.

If a piano is used for teaching a new song, play only the melody line. Piano or organ should never be played so loudly that the children's voices are drowned out. The adding of an accompaniment can best occur when the song has been learned well by the students. Rhythm instruments (sticks, tambourine, jingle bells, drums, rattles) can be made or purchased for use by students to accompany their singing. As children can't do two new things at once, use rhythm instruments only after the children know the song.

Encourage students to sing with their "happiest voices"; never ask them to sing "loud." Children encouraged to sing loudly will comply by shouting, and thus spoil the musical rendition and might possibly strain their vocal cords as well.

Children below the second grade do not need songbooks in their hands to learn to sing a song. Because they cannot yet read adequately, they are distracted by the songbook and are prevented from concentrating on the song leader.

Song leaders of very young children need to know that song learners come in two varieties. First, there are those who sing right off—at least their mouths are open and something is coming out! It is obvious that they are trying to learn the song, though we can hardly expect much precision in melody or words at this early stage. Each repetition of the song becomes a closer approximation to what it should be.

Then there are those other children! They will listen to a new song many times before they are confident enough to open their mouths at all. They may not even seem attentive, and teachers may feel that they are not even trying. But to tell them so might be a serious mistake; quite likely they are learning the song mentally. Such mental learners are often able to sing it perfectly the first time they open their mouths. Neither of these two varieties of learners has the edge in the speed of learning.

Action songs, in which arm and hand motions are correlated with the idea, can help children become involved before they can sing the song well. Rhythmic clapping also involves children at an early age. For example, the regular rhythm of "Jesus Loves Me" lends itself well to a beginning clapping experience. After that, songs with a slightly more complicated rhythm, such as "Praise Him," can be tackled.

For teachers of the youngest children for whom Sunday school may be their first singing experience, motivating all those "non-singers" may be the greatest challenge. Victor Hildner has written:

> For young children motivation is often related to people. A child first becomes interested in the teacher and then transfers that interest to the song which the teacher is teaching . . . Therefore the key to success in teaching music lies in the teacher's attitude.
>
> The effect of the teacher's attitude is immediate and direct. When a child hears a song enthusiastically and interestingly sung, he will instinctively follow a pattern which is common to all linguistic experiences: he will try to imitate. (*Joyfully Sing*, St. Louis: Concordia, 1961. P. xii)

Reading Scripture Publicly

The worship leader responsible for reading the Bible selection each Sunday has a serious responsibility. First, a choice must be made among the many translations available today. Should one use the same version in the Sunday school worship as was read in the regular service, or should the study Bibles used in the Sunday school be read? Certainly the version chosen should be one which students can readily understand. A sure way to turn children from use of the Bible is to give them the idea that it is too difficult for them.

The version chosen needs to be readable. The archaic words and out-of-date language of the King James Version even pose a problem for some adults. If a version cannot be read fluently and impressively, another translation should be chosen.

The cardinal rule for all public reading is to practice reading the selection aloud beforehand. Note the words to be emphasized to clarify the main idea of the selection. Find out the correct pronunciation of any word unfamiliar to you. No one can be impressed with the value placed on Scripture if the reader hesitates and stumbles through a few verses.

Although it is a good practice to involve students

occasionally in the public reading of the Scriptures, be sure that they practice in advance so they will read well. They might practice in the class session as well as at home.

Before you read the Scripture, get the reverent attention of the students. You might introduce the selection by giving them something for which to listen. Perhaps this could be a problem such as "Why should we give an offering to church?" Immediately following the reading, let the students discuss what the Scripture selection had to say about the problem posed.

Guiding Growth in Prayer

Many Sunday school students have memorized only table or bedtime prayers—if even that. Through memory work or regular use of new prayers in the worship session, Sunday school students can enlarge their repertoire of prayers to include also other occasions.

Further, Sunday school students need to gain experience in forming their personal prayers according to individual needs and conditions. To teach students how to frame a prayer of thanksgiving, you might ask the students to tell of blessings for which they are thankful. Then you might gather all the thoughts expressed by the students into one prayer of thanksgiving to serve students as a model. Or, you may say one phrase at a time, and give students time to repeat it before proceeding to the next phrase.

Prayers for the sick are another natural for children. Children may be able to pray by themselves for those whom they know. A worship leader who accepts completely all such early attempts at public prayer will effectively encourage further growth in this area.

The litany prayer form is simple enough to be introduced even to young children if the response expected from them has been made clear beforehand. In the following example, after each statement by the leader the students are to respond with the words, "Help us to obey our parents."

Versicles: In the Bible God says,
Honor your father and your mother.
To show that we love God. (Response)
Because we love our mothers. (Response)
Because we love our fathers.
(Response)

Response: Help us to obey our parents. Amen.

Older students can be introduced to the litany in its fullest expression, which includes an address to the Trinity, confession, intercessions, thanksgiving, and a conclusion in the name of Jesus. Some students may wish to write litanies themselves. If so, give the group a theme with which to work. Whenever appropriate, use these completed litanies. They may be sufficiently good to place in the church newsletter for use in homes of the parish.

Other informal types of prayers can encourage older children who have never expressed their thoughts to God in public. A sentence prayer works especially well because no one person is singled out but each one in turn speaks a short intercession. In the circle prayer, the leader prays last (or first to encourage others to pray). The circle prayer may lend itself better to the class session than to the devotion period because the class is smaller. Worshipers stand in a circle and join hands to symbolize the unity Christians find in prayer.

Prayer forms included in the worship resources of the church might also be introduced to older children. These would include the collects, the Lord's Prayer, and confessional prayers. The Lord's Prayer in particular ought to be memorized and understood by every student. The worship session is one setting in which this might be accomplished.

Too often prayers said in the worship session are perfunctory. With creative, thoughtful planning, the prayer portion of the session can become a meaningful worship experience and learning opportunity.

The Offering

Although the offering is a worship activity in which God's people express their gratitude and dedication by giving the Lord something of themselves, many people misunderstand this portion of the service. Some believe that the offering is for the pastor or worship leader. Others just do not know what the purpose is. Sunday school students can learn very early the significance and purpose of this worship action.

To visualize the fact that the offering is given to God for His work in the world through people, such as the church, let students drop their offerings into a slit cut into the top of a gift-wrapped box, or into a bank with Jesus' name on it. Discussions can be held occasionally to point out the purpose of the offering. Financial officers of the congregation might meet with older students to inform them how the offerings are used for the mission and ministry of the congregation.

Specific projects might be chosen to teach students of the worldwide mission of the church and to give them opportunity to contribute. Such projects are especially helpful if the students themselves choose the particular cause they want to support. Give time to describe some of the work being done through that chosen project.

Students might be taught that we can give the Lord more than money; we can give Him the use of our talents for helping others. One plan would be to spend a portion of the worship period to describe some of the services they might give their church. These might run the gamut from inviting a neighbor to church or Sunday school to mending hymnals, from sending get-well cards to children in hospitals to washing the windows of the Sunday school rooms. After the description, ask students to write on a slip of paper what they might do and then place this slip in the offering plate. This kind of project can make clear that in our offering we give ourselves in the money or pledge as a symbol of our life and our work.

Educating for the Church's Mission

Many Sunday schools give a worship period periodically to the purpose of informing students of the worldwide mission of their church. Mission fields and their needs can be described in many different ways. Speakers direct from a mission field of the church are probably the best resource. Motion pictures of the church's mission fields can be rented for projection. Book reports by a teacher or by students can help. Even toy people, houses, and vehicles can be used with younger children to visualize a mission project. Mission fairs can be sponsored by the Sunday school to inform students and others in the congregation of the work of their church.

You will want to give students opportunity to respond to the mission presentation. Perhaps the offering on that day can be designated for the worldwide missions of the church. Or, students might select a specific project they would want to support with their gifts. Students appreciate being involved in choosing where their mission offerings are to go. Decision-making is a necessity for adult Christians; the process can be learned already in Sunday school.

Training for Congregational Worship

Already early in life children can begin to prepare for worship with the congregation. Young children can learn to sing simple hymns, and such liturgical hymns as the *Gloria*

Patri. They can learn to pray the Lord's Prayer and possibly recite the Apostles' Creed.

Much more can be accomplished with older students. They can learn to understand the structure of the church's liturgies and the meaning of their various parts. Older children and youth can learn in Sunday school to sing the liturgical hymns in church and become acquainted with the hymnal. They also can learn many of the hymns of the church and perhaps even form a choir to sing in services.

Older children may learn the significance of the various liturgical actions such as facing the altar for prayer and the signing of the cross at certain points in the service. They can also be taught the significance of various symbols used in the church's architecture and appointments.

Older children and youth might well be taught the significance of each part of such occasional services as the Order of Holy Baptism.

Your pastor will be pleased to work with your Sunday school staff to develop a complete program extending over a number of years to prepare young people to become involved, informed participants of the worshiping community.

CONCLUSION

Worship is an essential part of your congregation's life. Your Sunday school in its worship sessions can contribute significantly to the development of your congregation as an informed, reverent worshiping community.

Chapter 4

How to Tell a Bible Story

Beverly Beckmann

Walk into just about any public library and you will be greeted by a sign that announces the date and time of "Story Hour." Most people assume that this refers to a story time for young children—and in most cases it does. However, the term "storytelling" does not apply to a technique for little children only, but is an art for all ages. Storytelling is a step beyond reading and is an exciting technique which can make a story live for any age.

For just that reason the art of storytelling should be explored by all people, but especially those involved in teaching the faith.

THE BIBLE STORY IN CHRISTIAN EDUCATION

For many years much religious education involved a funnel approach to teaching a Bible story. Bible truths were poured into the heads of youngsters much as milk is poured through a funnel into a bottle. Adults assumed that the children would listen and be able to repeat *back* the story. Their retelling would verify that they had indeed learned the story.

Times have changed along with educational philosophies. As instructors learn more about those they teach, their approaches have changed. Those who teach the faith have also changed their teaching views and approaches. We realize more clearly that youngsters must be responsible for their own learning. We can not do things *for* children, such as pouring knowledge into their heads. We cannot control or manipulate students so that they behave and think as we do. Teaching the faith certainly involves knowledge of the Bible—but with this knowledge also the feeling that God's story is *our* story.

The art of storytelling plays an integral part in imparting that story to others. John Westerhoff sums up this thought as follows: "Storytelling needs to become a natural and central part of church life, and we must learn to tell God's story as *our* story. No longer can we explain how some Israelites were once in bondage in Egypt and God saved them (who cares?). Instead we need to explain how *we* were once oppressed in Egypt and how God liberated *us*. We must again become a history-bearing community of faith and a storytelling people who seek to communicate God's story as our story." (John Westerhoff, *Will Our Children Have Faith?* New York: Seabury Press, 1976. P. 75)

The outgrowth of this kind of telling will be Christians who value each life as equal before God, and who acknowledge the need of others in their life. The interaction process of the storyteller and the listener must be encouraged to underscore the feeling of *our* story and the desire to share it with others.

Storytelling introduces the young child to the world of written language. A four-year-old may not be able to read the Bible, but the teacher who shares the contents of the Bible with her students builds in them a love for God's Word. The sharing process will continue as they become storytellers and share *their* story with their family and playmates.

THE ROLE OF THE STORYTELLER

Storytelling goes back to the beginning of time and was the means of passing history from one generation to the other. There are many advantages of storytelling which other forms of communication such as reading do not have.

Storytelling does not involve technology. Nothing comes between the narrator and the audience. Because of this, storytelling becomes a reciprocal interaction between the teller and the audience. The audience reacts to the teller and the storyteller in turn reacts to the audience. A personal relationship is built up between the two.

In addition, storytelling produces an immediate response from the audience. A storyteller can immediately ascertain whether his methods and content are producing excitement in the audience. If not, he can vary his approach.

Storytelling is a flexible skill. Each time the story is told, it can be modified to suit the vocabulary and attention span of the audience.

Storytelling is portable. All the equipment can be obtained at a moment's notice. Also, a storyteller can maintain eye contact and effectively influence the group. This cannot be done readily by reading the story.

Are you ready to be a storyteller? Here are a few guidelines to help.

1. Know the story. Be sure that you have the details clear in your mind. This takes advance preparation.
2. Know your audience. Be aware of their vocabulary, attention span, and background. Avoid "talking down" to them.
3. Enjoy the story. Unless you show a genuine love for the story, you will lose your audience. If a storyteller does not have any enthusiasm for the material, why should the listener? "You don't need a good voice, dramatic training, a spontaneously creative imagination, a movie

star's looks, or an elephant's memory." (John Lee Sherman, "Storytelling with Young Children," *Young Children,* January 1979, page 22). What you do need is enthusiasm.

4. Identify with the characters to communicate the spirit and feeling of the story. Try to feel their responses to situations. This will require some understanding of the Biblical times in which the story occurred. Many times this is provided in the teaching material for the course and is a vital part of the storyteller's background. Visualize the setting and characters. Try to imagine yourself at the birth of Jesus if that is the story. If you were a shepherd, how would you feel?
5. Be sensitive to textures, patterns, and rhythms to convey details to the children. It is important to know the beautiful colors in Joseph's coat and the sweet smell of the straw in Jesus' manger.
6. Vary the tone and pitch of the voice. If the listeners become restless, lower your voice to a whisper. Slowly build the volume as you reach the climax of the story. Use the pause to gain attention or gather your thoughts.
7. Call attention to the story and not to yourself. You are the tool whom God is using to convey His message. The story is the important thing. Don't become too dramatic or you will overshadow the story. Gestures should be subtle and not overpowering.
8. Maintain eye contact while telling the story. This lets your audience know that you are excited about what you are saying and you want them to hear it.
9. Realize that some children will say, "I've heard that before." This is not an insult to you or an indication of disrespect on the part of the listener. Tell the child to listen carefully and they may hear something new.
10. Do not memorize the story. Rather, read it through four

or five times. Try to visualize the story sequence in your mind. Know the plot, characters, and feeling of the story.

11. Always practice your story before presenting it to your audience.
12. Make sure that you are placed away from windows. It is difficult for the listener to watch the storyteller while glaring at a bright window.
13. As you tell the story, seat yourself so that you are on the same eye level as your students. Also, maintain direct eye contact with your students as you tell the narrative.
14. Be alert to the physical and emotional comfort of your students. They will enjoy the lesson more if they are physically comfortable and if they feel that they are accepted and loved by the teacher and other students.

TECHNIQUES AND DEVICES

Techniques and devices are used for three reasons. First of all, they can be used as an introduction to the story. We all need motivation and a feeling of anticipation as the story is about to be told. A creative introduction to the Bible story builds our anticipation for the content of the story.

Second, techniques facilitate the telling of a story. Flannelboards, for example, help the learner see the sequence of events in the story.

Third, a creative technique can be used by the learners to re-experience and re-enjoy what they have heard. These techniques excite children about the Bible story and cause them to enjoy that special time with their teacher. Devices such as flannelboards are not the sole property of the storyteller. They should be available for listener to try out. This will encourage the listener to become the story teller to others. This is our goal in teaching the faith. We are making all people fishers of men—sharers of the faith.

The following techniques and devices can be used by the storyteller and listener.

1. Attention getters
   a. Story bag. This can be either a plain paper bag or a fancy fabric bag with a draw string. It really doesn't matter what it looks like as long as it is used effectively. Place an item related to the story in the bag.
   b. Story hat. The storyteller could wear a special hat as the children arrive. It should contain a picture or an item related to the story tucked in the brim. A fish hook for the miraculous draft of fishes or a picture of a loaf of bread for the feeding of the 5000 is suggested. Children's interest will be aroused as to the lesson for the day and will be eager for the lesson to begin.
   c. Story apron. A bib-type apron would have a clear plastic pocket sewn on. Heavy vinyl can be purchased for this purpose. The pocket should be the size of the story leaflet so that the picture of the lesson is visible. The apron should be worn as you greet the class so that their curiosity is aroused by the picture. Older children will be able to read the title and begin to wonder about the story.
   d. Story house. A cardboard milk carton can be covered with felt to simulate a house. The peak portion becomes the roof. The windows can be made of felt which is glued on three sides only. The top is left open so that each window forms a pocket. In the pockets, pictures of the story characters (cut from leaflets) can be placed. The story house should be placed where the children can manipulate the figures and discuss them.
   e. Bulletin boards. A special section of the bulletin

board may be reserved for the "Story of the Week." Pictures and objects may be placed in the spot to indicate the topic of the story. For older children, the topic may be titled and accompanied by key phrases and pictures.

2. Object lesson
   a. Cross box. God's special gift to us is His Son. Six squares are taped together to form a cross. The reverse side is covered with gift-wrap paper. When folded together they form a box which can be tied with gift ribbon. The center portion of the cross should contain a picture of Christ.
   b. Clay. Clay can be molded to be the cave in which Jesus was buried and the stone rolled in front of it. Manipulate the clay as the story is being told.
   c. Color wheel. A color wheel can be used with younger children. It can be used to illustrate the colors in Joseph's coat or the creation story.

3. Flannelboard

The purpose of the flannelboard is to enlarge the story pictures. There are several don'ts to remember when using this device.

—Don't block the view of the flannelboard when telling the story.

—Don't talk to the board; talk to the listeners.

—Dont' use excessive movement of the pieces.

Many schools have flannelboards with tripods, but it is possible to make your own holder by covering a pizza board with felt and placing a loop of elastic on the back for a holder. The board is then held by the storyteller.

The pieces for the story can be from a prepared set or made by attaching felt to the back of pictures cut from previous leaflets. Others can be made from heavy Pellon and drawn on with felt tip markers.

The pieces should be placed in a pile in the sequence in which they occur. If several scenes are used, place the items in separate sections of a magazine so that they are kept separate.

4. Chalk talk

For a chalk talk, the storyteller draws while telling the story.

This technique is most effective if a large board is used. For small children, it is best if the board is near them. If a chalkboard is unavailable, have the students gather around a piece of paper and draw with a marker. An overhead projector is also effective for chalk talks.

Some people are very talented and can draw the scene to go with the story. But most people are not in that category and do not feel comfortable doing that. Then try the "easy chalk talk."

Decide what your finished product will look like. If you are telling the parable of the lost lamb, you may want to finish with a lamb. The narration then would consist of the shepherd realizing that his lamb was lost (as you draw a leg). So he went uphill and down (draw another leg) until his travels take him home and the lamb is completed. (This technique is further described in the study guide for this course.)

The idea of this type of chalk talk is to draw as you tell the story, but the objects are not the objects of the narrative. Simple stick objects are acceptable, and when the story is finished, it may look disorganized but each illustration or portion of the illustration has meaning while it is being done.

It is not necessray to be an artist to use this technique. It is not the finished product that is important, but the story that is being told as you do the drawing.

5. Cut talk

This technique is what the name implies. Either the main character or an object in the story is cut while the story is being told. It is easier if the object is drawn on the paper beforehand or if a folded paper is used. At Christmas time, tell the story of the birth of Jesus as you cut out one large heart and two small hearts from folded paper. Talk about how God loved us and sent us the baby Jesus. But where could baby Jesus sleep? The large heart becomes the manger and slots in the ends allow you to slip in the two smaller legs made of the smaller hearts.

Additional objects which are easy to cut are flowers for the lilies of the field or a tree for the parable of the fig tree.

6. Origami

Simple folded-paper techniques are effective for use with all ages. Many books are available on this technique which requires some amount of concentration. Those interested in it should refer to *Kirigami* by Frederick W. Kemper (St. Louis: Concordia, 1979).

7. Puppets

Many types of puppets, a popular device for telling stories, can be used. It is important to remember that you don't have to be a ventriloquist. An audience of any age becomes involved with the puppet and it is immaterial whether your lips move or not. Better yet, use an animal puppet to help tell the story. He can whisper the story in your ear. Then you can relate what he has told you with no voice attached to the puppet.

Types of puppets:

a. Sock. The heel of the sock forms the back of the head while the bottom forms the mouth.
b. Paper bag. The bottom of the closed bag forms the

top of the head. The hand inserted inside makes the mouth move. This can be drawn on easily with magic markers or crayons.

c. Finger puppets. Various Bible characters can be cut from old Sunday school leaflets. The bottom portion of the figure is cut off and holes for two fingers left. Fingers placed through the holes then make the legs of the puppet.

8. Rubbings

Key portions of the story can be drawn on paper. Then cover the lines with a thin trail of Elmer's glue. It takes about 24 hours for the glue to dry. Then cover the drawing with a sheet of newsprint. As the story is being told, rub over the drawing with colored chalk. The glue outline will appear as a heavy line of chalk.

9. Finger plays

Finger plays can be used as an introducton to the Bible story or as a followup at the end of the story. The following are sources of religious finger plays:

Margaret Self, *Creative Fingerfun* (Glendale, CA: Regal Books, 1974).

Finger Fun: Finger Plays and Action Games for Church Schools (Minneapolis: Augsburg, 1976).

INTERACTION OF STORYTELLER AND LISTENER

After telling the story, it is important to let the audience know that they too can be storytellers. The good news shared with one can spread to others. Use the following methods to encourage the audience to re-create the story.

1. Creative props

One of the easiest creative techniques to use in storytelling is use of a prop. A towel placed over the head and secured with a tie can create a shepherd; a cardboard box becomes the frankincense presented by the Wise Men. When using this method let the listeners know what is expected of them. If the audience is reluctant to participate, select a group of willing people to do the acting.

2. Tape recorder

Use a tape recorder to record the children's retelling of the story or record the various sound effects needed in the story.

3. Story on a roller

After telling the story, have each person draw a portion of the story. Decide on the correct sequence of the story and tape the pictures together. Or, draw directly on a roll of shelf paper. Place a roller (cardboard from toweling, or towel rod) and the students' script in a cardboard box. Members of the class can then retell the story as it reappears in the frame.

SOURCES OF MATERIALS

The best source of materials for telling stories is from previous leaflets in Sunday or weekday materials. Never discard pictures or leaflets. The following are some suggested uses for these pictures to be used in storytelling.

1. Puzzles

Glue the picture to a heavy piece of cardboard. Cut in large shapes for small children and more complicated patterns for older students. Vary the outer shape of the puzzle. For example, a heart puzzle is appropriate for Valentine's Day and a cross shape for Easter.

2. Peep box

Make a small hole at the end of a covered shoebox. Cut out a portion of the lid away from the peep hole and cover with wax paper. Place a picture at the end of the box opposite the hole. Prior to telling the story, encourage the children to look through the hole. Younger children can be challenged not to tell anyone what they see. Then have them whisper the secret to their neighbor.

3. Matching game

Cut apart a picture in two sections. The stories from several weeks should be used for this game. Then have the students match the pictures so that the halves are complete. Encourage telling the story after the pictures have been completed.

4. Maze

Prepare a maze on a large sheet of paper. Make it simple for the younger children and very complicated for the older ones. Place pictures from a Bible story at various spots along the maze. Encourage traveling from the beginning of the maze to the end as the student recalls the events in the story. This can be done as a group activity with spontaneous sharing of the Bible story.

CONCLUSION

Storytelling is an ancient art. It has proven to be effective for passing on history from one generation to another. Now let us use this same technique to pass on *our* story—God's love in Jesus Christ given by the power of His Spirit—from one generation to the next.

Chapter 5

How to Involve the Learner

Keith A. Loomans

WE ARE INVOLVED!

The learner is involved! Regardless of age, the learner is involved in life and growing stronger or weaker in faith. Each Christian is daily involved in the Law-Gospel cycle in which the person is indicted by the Law for sin, cries for help (confession), is forgiven (absolution), and responds to God in praise and adoration.

That's the story of the lame beggar recorded in Acts 3. The man had a handicap since birth. Being a descendant of Adam he bears the mark of sin in time. Because of his condition he is dependent on others. He cries out for help. He looks to others to give him alms. That's all the world can give. The world cannot remove his affliction. He looks to Peter and John for the help of the world—alms, a handout. He gets more! He receives a God-given cure. "In the name of Jesus Christ the Nazarene—walk!" (New American Standard)

From that moment on, he was really involved. He entered the temple with Peter and John as he walked, leaped, and praised God.

That's the involvement of each Christian every day. And it is just as dramatic. Daily God the Holy Spirit renews each of His family. He grants each believer newness of life, strength, mercy, and peace beyond understanding.

THE ROLE OF THE CLASS

That's the life in which each baptized student is involved. Church school classes help all participants grow in their understanding of their relationship with God as class time affords the opportunity in a structured way to examine life now in the context of life then.

The class session offers the Christian time to come apart, or come together and reflect on "involvement"—his life in Christ. As participants see again and again their own identity in Adam and every descendant of Adam they are brought face-to-face with the Law and the knowledge that because "you have sinned you shall die." Man cannot save himself. There is nowhere to turn but to God. Because of involvement in God's family the student—the Christian—again hears the message of the Gospel, "I forgive you, you are mine." Involvement with God means renewal and the response is praise, adoration, and a commitment to more sincere discipleship. That's real involvement!

Because teachers want that message to live in each student they are concerned that there is also involvement in the class session when teachers are about "teaching the faith."

Class participation or involvement is not automatic. There are those who are always participating. Then, there are those who seem to be disinterested. Involvement may be active or passive. The learner may be the recipient of some action or emotional touch of another student or the teacher. Such a student is passively involved. By comparison we are all involved in receiving God's grace and mercy—a passive involvement—and we grow as a result. Learning happens through passive involvement.

Similarly, Christians are also instruments of God as proclaimers and bearers of His gifts. That is active involvement. In church school classes, teachers want to build on that active involvement.

THE ROLE OF THE TEACHER

The teacher is the key in this process. The teacher is a shaper and molder of understandings, attitudes, and behaviors. The teacher designs the class sessions so that things happen in students. When students are "doing" they are more apt to learn. Therefore, it is a necessary part of lesson planning to devise and select ways to involve the learner in active participation.

There are a variety of ways for the teacher to involve students in faith building and enriching activities. Such a list would include simulation games, games which parallel life situations and create the kinds of tensions which are found in everyday life. The information and the feelings which are raised by the game are then processed for application to the Bible lesson or Scriptural teaching. The teacher may also use drama, skits, and role playing for student involvement. Another way to involve students is in the pattern of visit-reflection-response. In this activity teachers would involve students in a field trip or watch a movie, filmstrip, videotape, or involve them in some kind of encounter with a resource person which would be followed by a reflection period, a time for discussing what had been observed. On the basis of this discussion there would be individual or group response. An example might be as follows: the class studies one of the Biblical narratives dealing with how God cares for people. As a way of emphasizing that God acts through people the teacher would plan a visit to a local nursing home to allow students the opportunity to visit with residents and share their faith through song and conversation. After the visit the group would discuss their reactions, what they had learned, and how they felt, and then relate this to God's plan of care for people. In response to the visit and reflection the group might decide to do this on a regular basis. It may also be the case that individuals will plan other activities whereby they would be involved on a regular basis with someone who is in need of care.

Additional ways for teachers to involve students would be through the use of conversation groups, encounter groups, small-group sharing, problem-solving sessions, values clarification exercises, debates, case studies, listening to cassette tapes, preparing a slide presentation, puppetry, and others.

THE ROLE OF DISCUSSION

While each of these will provide some degree of physical and mental involvement, the activity is not complete without discussion to relate the activity to the theme and goals of the lesson. Discussion may be as simple as a few moments spent on clarification of a point of the lesson or may be as complex as assisting participants in organizing learnings into a value system.

Teachers use discussion to reinforce important truths or to correct inaccurate impressions. Skillful teachers use discussion at times to gain attention of students. At other times the teacher guides a student into participation through a discussion process.

The teacher will manage and facilitate the discussion in such a way that students will make personal application and be open to sharing their insights.

THE ROLE OF STUDENTS

The teacher must realize that good discussion doesn't just happen in a class. Students will have to be trained in the discussion process. Aspects of a good discussion are listening, respecting the opinions of others, exercising personal responsibility for sharing one's own ideas, and using time wisely. Listening is not to be equated with hearing. People hear sounds all about them but may not be concentrating on what they are hearing. Listening involves paying attention to the speaker. Participants in discussion have to fight the temptation to prepare their next speech while the other person is talking. An intelligent response to a previous statement requires careful listening to what is being said.

Students need to learn to respect the opinions of others. So often there is the tendency to put down the other person for what has been said. Each person is entitled to an opinion. There is also a responsibility that if the expressed opinion is challenged and the person can be shown where he or she is wrong, then it becomes the responsibility of that person to change their opinion. The teacher must monitor this process so that the dialogue or debate is done in a caring manner.

In a discussion it is the responsibility of each participant to share one's own ideas. Often the teacher will hear a student say later that "I wasn't given a chance to say what I wanted to say." The teacher will try to get every participant involved but can hardly read a person's mind to know that someone who doesn't speak up has something to say. So, the teacher should periodically remind students that when they have something to say they should say it. Moreover, the teacher must create an accepting climate so students are encouraged to express themselves.

SOME KEYS TO GOOD DISCUSSION

Good discussion depends on wise use of time. The teacher should guide the discussion so that it stays on the topic. Time is often lost when the discussion gets off on a tangent. Students should be informed regarding the amount of time available for the discussion. The teacher should help the group use the time wisely.

The teacher will not only have lesson goals but will also have some process goals, e.g., more students are talking, or more students are sharing personal insights, or students are asking more questions of each other.

Teachers should be aware of class interactions. Is the teacher the only one asking questions? After the teacher asks the questions are there a number of student reactions? Are students talking to and asking each other questions? Is the teacher in the role of guiding discussion, or is the teacher having to work to keep the discussion alive?

A good student-teacher interaction pattern in the discussion is one like the following: Teacher asks question, student one responds, student two reacts, student three adds a comment, one of the students asks a question or shares a comment followed by another student, etc. When the students are activley involved the chances for learning to take place are greatly enhanced. One way to evaluate teacher-student interaction is to tape record the discussion; later the teacher listens to a playback of the tape to record the order in which people talk. Who talks the most? If the recording shows that the teacher is doing most of the talking, the teacher will want to make some changes. If the recording indicates that after a question by the teacher only one student responds, the teacher may want to review the types of questions being asked. From the recording the teacher will also be able to determine how well the group is adhering to the topic of discussion.

Interaction analysis can be very helpful in improving the quality of class discussion. Good discussion process doesn't just happen. It takes work on the part of the teacher and students. Since discussion is usually introduced and maintained by questions, the quality of the discussion will depend on the quality of the questions. So, it is important that the teacher have a knowledge of questions and develop good questioning skills.

THREE TYPES OF QUESTIONS

Questions can be categorized in a variety of ways, but there are basically three types: informational, analytical, and personal. Informational questions are the kind which can be answered "yes" or "no," with a single fact, or with a factual statement. For this reason informational questions are called *closed* questions.

Analytical and personal questions are called *open* questions because there is the potential for a variety of responses. A sample informational question would be: Why was Daniel thrown into the lion's den? An analytical question growing out of this same story would be: Why do you think Daniel disregarded the law and prayed to God? An example of a personal question would be: What would you have done if you had been in Daniel's place?

All three types of questions are necessary for a good discussion. Informational questions alone will not foster a meaningful discussion. Yet informational questions are necessary when working with cognitive goals pertaining to recall and comprehension, and to some extent at the application, analysis, and synthesis levels.

Analytical questions require some thinking before a response is given. The analytical question is a tool in discussion relating to cognitive (knowledge) goals of application, analysis, and synthesis, to affective (emotional, feeling) goals of appreciation and attitudes.

Personal questions are also *open* questions which involve students in relating lesson material to personal life. The personal question helps the student in a reflection and response process to progress from understanding to attitude development (organization of a value system) and behavior change (decision-making based on a maturing Christian understanding of life).

Effective use of these three types of questions will help students reach higher levels of both cognitive (knowledge) and affective (emotional) goals.

PURPOSE OF QUESTIONS

The areas in which the question serves as an important involvement tool are: (1) to introduce a new subject; (2) to stimulate discussion of a familiar subject; (3) to review lesson material; (4) to reflect on some personal experiences; (5) to apply a Bible subject to some personal experiences; (6) to interpret Bible passages; (7) to motivate further research; (8) to discuss a film, filmstrip, cassette tape or other media; (9) to explore a subject more deeply; (10) to analyze a personal or social problem; (1) to brainstorm solutions to a problem; (12) to conduct an interview either by an actual interview or by roleplaying; (13) to clarify values expressed by a person; (14) to explore beliefs or commitments; (15) to challenge a thesis or statement; (16) to evaluate how lesson activities relate to goals; and others.

QUESTIONING TECHNIQUES

Effective questioning requires good questioning techniques. A teacher should spend enough planning time to phrase questions properly. It is a good idea to rehearse (speak out loud) the questions to be used. The strength of the question is not only in the words used but also in word emphasis and voice inflection. People are entranced by skilled storytellers. Students are more apt to respond to well-worded and well-intoned questions.

Teachers are encouraged to ask more open than closed questions to stimulate thoughtful participation. In lesson preparation the teacher should review the quality of the questions of his or her own—write these questions out. The teacher should also anticipate what questions might be raised by students or what direction the discussion might take so that good extemporaneous questions can be phrased. Good questioning takes practice. The teacher should keep asking "why" questions—why do you think . . . ?; or "how" questions—how would you have acted . . . ?; or "what" questions—what would you do next? Or, what could have been done?

Present one question at a time. If it is necessary to rephrase the question, be careful not to add something to change the direction of the question. Some students are already in the thought process and a change can cause confusion.

Make it a point to ask questions only one time. Demand that kind of attention. Then give time for students to think. If a question is worth asking it will require "thought time." After asking the question, wait for a student to answer. Sometimes there will be a long period of silence. Wait the students out. After the teacher asks a question, the next one to speak should be the student. If the teacher breaks the silence the teacher is in fact teaching the class members that they don't have to answer. Some teachers answer their own questions rather than lose time. Although time is precious in a class session, it is not so precious as to lose out on the opportunity to help students understand that their involvement in the discussion raises the quality of that discussion. Teachers want the lesson experience to be as meaningful as possible in individual lives and therefore will patiently seek active student involvement.

The teacher should follow through on responses with probing questions. Students should be encouraged to ask questions of each other and of the instructor. Through probing questions students can be led to a deeper understanding of the lesson material and its application to life.

Questions should be presented to the whole class. All members should engage the question. Some teachers are tempted to use questions as a means for maintaining attention or for controlling a person or group. If a person is called upon to answer before the question is posed, the other students are notified that they don't have to do any thinking on "this one." Too often a student is singled out in this way for a "put down" by the teacher and the class, e.g., "If you would have been paying attention, you would know the answer." Questions are tools to aid quality discussion rather than to discipline students.

Teachers should use questions which "inquire" or engage students rather than "grill" or interrogate them. "Grilling" of the class arouses discomfort or hostility and defeats the positive purposes of group discussion.

Some teachers have a habit of echoing (mechanically repeating) student responses. Not only does this irritate some people but it also wastes time. Repeat an answer only if you can determine by the facial expressions of students that others in the group did not hear or do not understand the reply. You may repeat a student's answer or response to underline or emphasize a point in an effective way. Have a definite purpose whenever you repeat an answer; do not merely echo indiscriminately all responses.

Students will sometimes give similar answers or echo a previous speaker. Train students to listen while another is speaking or giving an answer. Encourage them to add additional information or comments without merely repeating what has been said.

Treat all student responses with kindness and respect. Receive each answer to a question as a gift. After a student response provide some kind of positive feedback to indicate that you appreciate the response, even if it is a wrong reply.

When a student gives a wrong answer, indicate that it is not the answer to the question you just asked and phrase a question to fit the answer. Don't say anything to stifle future participation. In this way the teacher can set a positive example for students in their relationships to persons who give wrong responses.

YOUR CHALLENGE

As a teacher in the church you want your students to grow in their Christian faith and life. The Holy Spirit accomplishes this growth also through your teaching of the Word of God. Through your teaching the Holy Spirit would not only lead your students into a deeper understanding of His message as He has given it to us in the Scriptures, but He would lead your students into a closer relationship with their God, nourish them in their faith, strengthen their commitment to their Lord and His church, and empower them to live as God's people in the world.

If learners are to grow, they themselves must be involved in the learning process. To guide students in their involvement, you as teacher need to understand the discussion process and to sharpen your skills in good questioning techniques. A careful reading of this chapter can help you become not merely a teller of God's story, but a guide to your students as they actively explore through questions and discussions the truths of God.

Chapter 6

How to Use Audiovisuals

Hal H. Whelply, Jr.

WHY USE AUDIOVISUALS?

Audiovisuals are the basis of effective and efficient teaching in today's church school. That may seem to be a strong statement, even an overstatement. However, if you believe anything less to be true of audiovisuals (AVs), your students are probably missing rich learning opportunities.

For many years AVs have been called audiovisual aids. That term is unfortunate because "aids" may suggest that AVs are optional. Many people believe that "audiovisual aids" are a change of pace, something to grab student attention, and, incidentally, present some lesson content—but optional nevertheless. They think that real teaching occurs when the teacher lectures or explains the material to be learned. Audiovisual aids exist solely as accessories in the teaching process.

In fact, AVs should and can be far more than merely optional accessories. AVs are tools as essential for the teacher as a hammer and saw are for the carpenter.

The essence of the teacher's role is to bring the student and the learning task together in such a way that the student can successfully accomplish the task in the most effective and efficient manner. In other words, the teacher's job is to help the student learn as thoroughly and as quickly as possible. The teacher who believes that this is done primarily through lecturing to students and asking questions is deceiving himself. He is limiting himself to the use of one teaching tool when several are needed to do the job.

There are two major reasons why today's church school teacher should use a variety of teaching tools. First, any class includes a variety of individuals with different learning styles. Some do learn quite well from listening to a teacher. Others must see actual objects or pictures to comprehend an idea. Many find it most necessary to *do* something, to build, form, paint, and so on. They must handle and manipulate things. Of course, none of us has the luxury of learning in our preferred style all the time. However, the effective teacher acknowledges and respects the learning style preferences of all her students in *some* way *some* of the time. The use of AVs provides the teacher with alternative tools for meeting learning style needs.

Second, any class today includes students who are already quite accustomed to using a variety of AVs in their daily lives. Church school teachers are not different. You might ask yourself which of the following are a part of your life at work or at home:

Television (and videocassette or videodisc players)
Radio (AM, FM, CB, etc.)
Telephone
Computer
Audio tape recorder (cassette, dictation equipment, etc.)
Phonograph (stereo)
Electronic calculator
Movies
Camera (instant print, 35mm, TV, x-ray machine, etc.)
Photocopy machine (also a type of camera)
Microform readers (microfilm, microfiche, etc.)

Photographs (snapshots, x-rays, slides, etc.)
Typewriters

Chances are that you and your students live in a world abounding in audiovisual messages, and the equipment to produce and play them. Students who live in such a highly audiovisual environment are handicapped in a church school where the teacher is the main AV.

AV equipment and materials are gifts of God. The tools available to us for communicating the Gospel in church school settings have power beyond that even dreamed of in earlier days. The fact that God provides such tools to us in our age may say something about our task. Can we afford not to use what He has given us?

GUIDELINES FOR AV USE

Much can be accomplished through the use of AVs; however, it is necessary, as with all things, to maintain proper perspective in this area as well. The following are general guidelines for appropriate AV use.

1. *Don't overuse AVs.* Relying on AVs too much can numb student minds as thoroughly as too much lecturing. If your class sessions consist of a filmstrip, a movie, and a recorded hymn followed by the Lord's Prayer and benediction, you need to reassess your style. There is a vast difference between impersonal lecturing on the content of a lesson, and genuine discussion. Effective use of AVs can help avoid the shortcomings of lecturing, but should not impinge upon good discussion. In our intensely audiovisual world, one of our greatest church school needs is for warm, caring Christian teachers who really *listen* to their students. If your use of AVs prevents caring discussion and listening, you are overusing AVs.

2. *Just because an AV is an audiovisual does not mean*

you should use it. Before using an AV with your class, preview it at least once, preferably twice. You know your students—something of their personal lives, their intersts, their abilities, and their learning styles. The commercial producers of the AV you're considering did not know *your* students when they designed the AV. When it comes to your class, you are the expert. You decide if the AV is the right one for your group.

3. *Select, make, and use AVs on the basis of clear objectives.* Don't use an AV merely because it seems to treat the same general area your lesson covers, or simply because it is available. Use AVs because you have evaluated them and decided they will help to achieve the objectives you have set.

4. *A professionally-produced AV is not necessarily more effective than one you produce.* Don't be intimidated by professional slickness. Perhaps you are not able to produce a polished, sophisticated AV. But the audio cassettes and overhead transparencies you make will probably meet your students' needs better than anything you could buy because you produced them with your students in mind.

5. *Seek quality in visual compositions.* Too often most, if not all, of the instructional content in AVs is contained in the sound track, or the verbal material to accompany the visuals. However, visuals should also work in conveying the instructional message. Visuals and sound should constitute an integral whole in such a way that the message is incomplete unless both are present.

Good visuals communicate concepts clearly. Composition is relatively simple, with only necessary details included. Line drawings (e.g., of a mechanism) are usually easier to understand than photographs of the actual item. Thus, simplicity, an uncluttered composition which presents essentials, is generally to be valued over realism. In most cases, "one concept per visual" is a safe and prudent rule-of-thumb.

6. *Get to know your AV equipment.* Familiarity with AV equipment is not quite enough. You should become *comfortable* with it so that there is almost no chance of a surprise that you cannot deal with (short of a malfunction requiring professional repair). Such intimate knowledge of your AV equipment will probably result in fewer "breakdowns" because, given modern equipment which has not been abused, most breakdowns are due to errors in operation and not machine malfunction.

7. *Involve students in making and using AVs.* Why should student responses to learning God's Word be limited to recitation or filling in blanks in lesson booklets? Student-made slides, audio recordings, overhead transparencies, and the like, can be a vibrant testimony to the faith which some may find difficult to verbalize. Furthermore, students cannot be really involved in making AVs without being involved in learning.

8. *Plan ahead.* You probably know Murphy's Law: If anything can go wrong, it will. Most of us have experienced that law in action. By involving yourself and students with AVs you are introducing more complexity, and, thereby, more opportunities for things to go wrong. In the long run it is worth the risk because there are also more opportunities for learning to occur. Before introducing an activity, try it yourself. You will be able to anticipate potential problems and avoid them. Through careful planning, Murphy's Law can usually be effectively neutralized.

USING OVERHEAD TRANSPARENCEIS

The overhead projector (OP) is one of the least complicated audiovisual devices, yet one of the most useful. The OP projects the images on what could be called a large, clear slide, about the size of a sheet of typing paper, known as a *transparency*. The OP has been called the "electric chalkboard," and with good reason.

Advantages of Overhead Transparencies

1. You face your students and maintain eye contact as you present material on the OP; you do not need to turn your back on the class to write new material as you must when using a chalkboard.

2. The OP projects transparencies in a normally lighted room. There is no need for concern about closing shades or draperies.

3. Transparencies can be prepared in advance for smooth, sequential presentation. There is no tedious writing on the limited area of a chalkboard, repeated erasing and more writing.

4. The information on transparencies is visible only when you want it to be; attention can be directed to or from the information by use of the OP power switch. Further control is possible by obstructing light passing through the transparency with a piece of paper. You move the paper to reveal additional information as you are ready.

How to Use Overhead Transparencies

The overhead transparency is so versatile that its use is limited only by one's imagination. Here are some suggestions to spark your own ideas. Remember that the suggestions can apply to both teacher and student use.

1. Illustrate a Bible story with drawings on transparencies. You need not be an artist; simple stick figures will do. Or, trace the major outlines from pictures in curriculum materials or magazines. Try tracing parts of various pictures of similar proportions on the same transparency to piece together new illustrations (e.g., Jesus from one picture, a child from another, etc.).

2. Use transparencies as you would a chalkboard to present questions, Bible passages, hymns or songs, prayers, role-playing situations, and so on. Prepare them in advance or, if the quantity of material is brief, write on transparencies during your presentation.

3. Trace maps on transparencies. Show routes as they develop in Bible narratives, e.g., Paul's journeys.

4. Project transparency "banners" as the focus for a worship theme, or, with a simple altar, as "instant" worship centers.

5. Illustrate a story with overhead projection puppets. For silhouette puppets, cut simple character shapes out of opaque paper, e.g., construction paper. Draw a scenery backdrop on a transparency, and act out the story with the puppets on top of the transparency. Or, draw puppets with transparency pens on a piece of transparency film. Allow extra film at the bottom to which a popsicle-stick handle can be taped. Act out the story on the bare projector stage.

6. Use colored cellophane, tapes, markers, and other suitable materials to create a collage. The idea is to combine colors, lines, shapes and textures to convey moods or feelings, or other-worldly experiences difficult to imagine (e.g., creation).

7. Lift pictures from major magazines (e.g., *Time*, *Newsweek*, etc.). Obtain clear Con-Tact self-adhesive plastic. Cut a piece slightly larger than the desired picture to allow for mounting. Apply it smoothly, without bubbles or creases, and very thoroughly to the picture. Soak the paper/plastic combination in water to which you have added a few drops of dishwashing detergent. The paper will soak off, leaving the picture ink embedded in the adhesive on the plastic, just as it appeared on paper. Rinse the transparency, using a cotton ball to gently swab away any paper residue clinging to the plastic. After the transparency is dry, a thin

coat of clear plastic spray (e.g., Krylon) will afford protection and make the film more transparent. Mount the transparency on a frame.

USING FILMSTRIPS

Filmstrips are short lengths of 35mm film like that used in movie theater projectors. Instead of showing 24 frames (pictures) per second to create the illustion of motion, the filmstrip projector is used to show one frame at a time. The filmstrip, especially when accompanied by sound, is a very useful AV for several reasons.

Advantages of Filmstrips

1. Filmstrips are an easily-stored, economical means of providing high quality visuals in a carefully structured sequence.
2. Filmstrip projectors or viewers are easy to operate and many models are relatively inexpensive. Synchronized-sound projectors automatically advance the filmstrip for effective presentations that rival movies in instructional value and appeal.
3. Filmstrips can be used for individual, small-group or large-group instruction or worship.
4. Inexpensive frosted "write-on" filmstrip material can be used to create handmade filmstrips.

How to Use Filmstrips

1. Show a filmstrip to introduce, provide an overview, or review a Bible story, a topic, or a unit. Learning will be enhanced if, prior to the showing, you (a) tell students what the filmstrip is about; (b) describe how the topic relates to what the class is or will be studying; and (c) list two or three major points for which they should watch.
2. As a review activity, provide a filmstrip to students on the topic under study without the audio cassette or script.

Their task is then to write a script. The next step could be to record the narration.

3. Narrative filmstrips can be stopped in the middle so that students can write and discuss possible endings.

4. Using write-on filmstrip material, produce your own filmstrip on Bible narratives for which you have no other AV. Use colored markers, pens, and pencils.

5. Create a filmstrip parable to illuminate a Bible truth.

6. Illustrate and retell a Bible story from the viewpoint of someone who seems to have had a minor role (e.g., Simon of Cyrene).

7. Use selected visuals from a filmstrip to illustrate ideas presented on overhead transparencies.

USING SLIDES

Slides have come in many sizes over the years, up to 3¼″ by 4″. As mentioned earlier, the overhead transparency can be considered a large slide. The term "slide" here refers to what is often called the "standard 2 by 2 slide." Though its outer dimensions are 2″ by 2″, the standard slide may contain pieces of film of various sizes. Most slides are produced in 35mm cameras, and the visible film in such slides is approximately 1″ by 1½″ (24mm by 36mm).

Commercially available AVs for church school curricula rarely include slides. Filmstrips are usually more appropriate and less expensive. Therefore, the slides you use in church school will most likely be those you and your students make, whether in cameras or handmade.

Advantages of Slides

1. Slides are an easily stored, economical means of providing high quality visuals.

2. Slides are easily shown on simply operated pro-

jectors, and, with some additional coordination, on filmstrip projectors with slide adaptors.

3. Slides are useful for individual, small-group or large-group instruction or worship.

4. Inexpensive frosted "write-on" slides can be purchased or made (using the filmstrip material and slide mounts) to create handmade visuals.

5. Slides make possible infinite arrangements, additions and deletions in a visual sequence. Thus, a slide presentation is relatively easy to update or to adapt to various audiences.

How to Use Slides

1. Photograph students striking dramatic poses as they act out a Bible narrative.

2. Take pictures of familiar scenes around your neighborhood which are suitable as visuals to illustrate the reading of a psalm. The idea is to hear the psalm and see the scenes in a new light, to provide fresh insights into the Word.

3. Obtain write-on slides, or make your own from write-on filmstrip material and full-frame 35mm slide mounts. Produce hand drawn slides using overhead transparency pens, markers, pencils, etc. This is a good way to plan a photographic series before you shoot it. The process of using sketches to plan visuals is called "storyboarding."

4. Lift pictures from magazines with Con-Tact, as suggested for overhead transparencies. You will be surprised how many slide-size pictures, or suitable parts of pictures, can be found in magazines. Quality will not be as good as in overhead transparencies because you will be enlarging (through projection) a piece of film less than 1/40th the size of the overhead transparency so that it fills the same screen; however, it will be acceptable.

5. Recycle old vacation slides. Use them as they are (e.g., scenic slides) or moisten the less-shiny side slightly and scratch lines and patterns with a pin. Add color with markers. This scratch-and-color method, of course, lends itself to communicating moods or feelings (e.g., create visuals to accompany a reading of Psalm 150).

USING AUDIO CASSETTE TAPES

The audio cassette recorder is another remarkably versatile yet simply operated AV device. The recorder and cassette can be handled by all ages, from primary school up. An audio recording can be the complement to visual presentations, whatever the medium.

Advantages of the Audio Cassette

1. The cassette is small, easily stored, and durable.
2. Cassettes can be erased and re-recorded numerous times, thus making them one of the most economical AVs.
3. Audio recording is a potent motivator; students are fascinated by the process of recording and listening to their audio products.

How to Use the Audio Cassette

1. Create filmstrip or slide narrations. Simple sound effects can enhance recordings. For example, crinkling paper near the microphone can simulate the sound of crackling fire.
2. Produce a radio-style drama.
3. Conduct interviews. Bring Bible personalities to life in on-the-scene reporter interviews. Or, interview the pastor, someone of a different denomination, etc.
4. Use the recorder to listen to student memory work while you attend to other teaching tasks. Evaluate the recitation at your convenience.
5. Accompaniment for hymns and songs can be pre-

recorded for in-class use or for background music for use before class, during art or AV production sessions, etc.

6. Record a class period for the benefit of students unable to attend.

7. Record the script of a short puppet play you've written to present a Bible story. This frees your puppeteers to concentrate on manipulating their puppets during a performance.

USING FILMS AND VIDEO RECORDERS

The 16mm film, and the prerecorded videocassette or videodisc, are the most realistic AVs in that they combine visuals with motion and sound. As of this writing, most of the useful program material for church schools is in 16mm films. However, the next few years should provide a significant increase in the quantity and quality of resources in video.

Advantages of Films and Video Recordings

1. Films and video recordings can recreate real or imagined events useful in presenting factual information about Bible or church history.

2. These AVs present real life situations with which students can identify as they reflect on living their faith in such situations.

3. Film and video presentations overcome some differences in background and ability among students, allowing for discussion and increased understanding based on a common experience.

How to Use Films and Video Recordings

1. Effective use of film or video recordings ordinarily involves more than just viewing the presentation. It is important to prepare students for the experience, and to provide for sensitively guided discussion afterward. The

following general approach will serve well in most situations.

a) Begin in the manner suggested for filmstrips, i.e., tell the students what the presentation is about, how it relates to the unit or lesson, and what to watch for.

b) After viewing allow students to gather their thoughts and impressions. Provide time for them to deal with *what* they saw and heard, first. Avoid an immediate attempt to prove the possible meanings. Discussion could be sparked with a question such as: "What is one thing you saw or heard in the film which really stands out in your mind now?"

c) Next, deal with student feelings, values, and opinions. Elicit responses to questions like these: "How do you *feel* now about ______________________________ ? Which scenes do you think you'll remember a year from now?"

d) Then, draw out reflections on meanings. Lead students to interpretation through questions similar to these: "What does this film have to do with us? Of what does this film remind you in your own life? What does the film have to do with our Bible story?"

Your function as teacher is *not* to give a sermonette on the lesson the students should learn from the AV. Rather, your function is to enable and encourage student discussion.

2. Be selective about what and how a presentation is shown. If only a 10 minute segment in the middle of the film is of primary interest, show only that part. If it would be helpful to stop a videocassette at two points for further exploration, by all means do so. Films and videocassettes need not be shown from beginning to end or with teacher intervention.

3. Try leaving the sound off. Could students or teacher write and produce a sound track more appropriate for the

group's purposes? Use a phonograph or cassette player to add background music if desirable.

4. Stop a dramatic presentation before its resolution. Discuss possible endings. If appropriate, have students assume roles of film characters and roleplay the possible endings.

USING MAPS

Maps are of primary value in studying Bible history in intermediate and higher grade levels. Maps used should be simple, with only necessary detail. If a suitable map is not available, one may be produced by tracing the area of interest from an atlas on an overhead transparency. If an enlarged wall map is desired, the transparency can be projected on a sheet of paper and traced. The transparency can also be used in a copy machine to produce paper copies for students.

How to Use Maps

1. Superimpose an outline of your city, county, state, etc., on the map of Bible lands you are studying so that students may compare known geography to the unfamiliar and thereby better appreciate size and distance. Of course, it is important to use maps with the same scale. Outline the Bible lands on one transparency with one color, and draw your local area on another transparency in another color. Project both at the same time.

2. Use a map as a review device. For example, students may trace the path of the Israelites in the wilderness in terms of events and locations indicated in the Scriptural account.

3. Relate the Bible land area under study to current events. Superimpose a map of present political boundaries on the geographical realities of the Bible times under study.

Again, use two overhead transparencies. Point out contemporary names for the area.

USING POSTERS

Posters are like outdoor billboards, except in size. Their function is a bold, graphic, attention-grabbing presentation of a single theme or idea. Usually their message is directed at arousing feelings or changing attitudes.

Posters are useful in the church school because they are inexpensive and serve to focus student attention on an issue. Posters are a mode of communication students understand and appreciate; they are commonly used to decorate students' bedrooms. If produced by students themselves, they force direct confrontation with the issue at hand if the desired message is to be captured in poster style.

How to Use Posters

1. Discuss the poster, using the following basic approach.

   a) What is pictured in the poster? A poster artist must be very selective in what he includes in a design; thus, each element in the design is there for a purpose. Use the overhead projector to list these elements as students mention them.

   b) What do the pictured items represent? List the symbols possibly intended in the visual elements identified.

   c) What do the symbols mean? What idea was the artist attempting to convey by selecting and using the visual elements as he did?

   d) What feeling does the poster convey? What is your general feeling toward its message?

2. If no words are included in the design, have students decide what would be appropriate. Suggest a maximum

number of words, perhaps 10.

3. Use the poster as a centerpiece for a collage which builds and enlarges upon the poster theme. Obtain related visuals from magazines. Mount the poster on a large sheet of paper, and use the wide borders so provided to support collage materials around the poster.

4. Use a poster accompanying your curriculum material to inspire student-designed posters on the same theme.

5. Students may develop a series of posters (one per student) based on the apostles, parts of the catechism, books of the Bible, heroes of faith, and so on.

CONCLUSION

As a church school teacher, you want to present the Gospel of Jesus Christ as attractively and compellingly as possible. Today you have the choice of a wide variety of tools to use to accomplish this. Wise use of AV can strengthen your teaching and provide a wide variety in lesson presentation to compel attention and to share the Gospel effectively.

Chapter 7

How to Teach Memory Work

Donald A. Rosenberg

WHY MEMORY WORK?

"How To Teach Memory Work" is an unusual title for a chapter in a current book on teaching methods. Recent editions of the *Encyclopedia of Educational Research* have no entries for "memory" or "memorization." A survey of professional magazines uncovered only four articles on memorizing. Since all of them were a plea for memorization, it is quite obvious that limited rote memorization is taking place in secular education.

The neglect of memorization as a teaching-learning process is also reflected in the Lutheran school curriculum. The 1943 *General Course of Study for Lutheran Elementary Schools* contains nine pages on memory work. Included are suggestions to the student, suggestions to the teacher, suggestions for recitation, and aids in studying a lesson. The 1964 *Curriculum Guide for Lutheran Elementary Schools* contains less than one-half page on teaching memory selections. It includes this significant statement: "This guide will not demand a formal memory course at every age level, though teachers can, of course, continue to use such available programs."

The July/August, 1970 issue of *Interaction* includes comments from four respected educators in an article entitled, "The Great Memory Work Debate." A ballot was included at the end of the article and readers were encouraged to vote their preferences. The results of the ballot and excerpts from letters were published in the November, 1973 issue of *Interaction*. The results of the ballot were as follows:

No formal memory work	4%
Some, but less than we have now	39%
More than we have now	39%
A lot more than we have now	11%
Other responses	7%

The unknown factor in the survey is how much memory work was being taught in the parishes where teachers responded to the survey. One conclusion that could be drawn from the survey was that many teachers were dissatisfied with the memory work course of study that was being used in their parish at the time of the survey. From my observations, I suspect that a survey today would produce similar results.

The controversy over the place of memory work in the teaching of religion has continued for as long as I can remember. There is not a topic which has caused more heated debate in Christian education than memory work. Authorities can be quoted on both sides of the issue. Most of the arguments about memory work have created more heat than light.

Rote memorizaton of subject matter was the accepted teaching-learning process during the 19th century, although even then there were periods of negative reactions. When a growing volume of educational research indicated that there was a limited retention of memorized materials, this teaching method declined in popularity. Many people in Christian education also became disenchanted with memory work. People who had difficulty memorizing turned against religion and the church because of the harsh methods and punishments which were sometimes used when teaching memory selections.

Some of the research on the rate of forgetting memorized Bible verses tends to verify the limited value of rote memorization. In 1959 Rev. William Adam surveyed 108 youth at a Walther League rally in northern Indiana. Only 51% of the memorized materials were retained 6 months after confirmation and only 19% five years after confirmation. In a similar survey of Sunday school teachers, only 37% of the memorized materials were retained.

Proponents of memory work say, "So what! We keep much other content in the curriculum when the rate of forgetting is just as great." They point to many people who have found joy and comfort from recalling Bible, catechism, and hymn selections in times of danger, temptation, sickness, and old age. Supporters of memorization are also found in secular education. Elizabeth Compiglia wrote, "Every professional has memorized. The typist knows the keyboard; the chemist, valences; the carpenter, measurements. A good policeman knows the streets of the city and the doctor memorizes many symptoms and procedures." William Hastings, Associate Professor of Psychology at Monmouth College, stated, "Committing information to memory is a mature, practical, and creative activity that is integral to education at all levels." Ernest Hilton's editorial in the December, 1975, *Instructor*, comments, "But there comes a time when the facts must be committed to memory. Any child who has to discover them over and over, plainly is handicapped."

Jean Mizer Todhunter, author of "Cipher in the Snow," presents strong arguments for memorization. She writes, "No sensible teacher would contend that the old rote memorization, the meaningless parroting back of meaningless gunk, has the slightest value. But to make a great idea, a great line, a part of yourself, that is a highly different thing." She comments further, "Great ideas, great concepts, great words can be understood and used as intellectual tools by any competent student reader, but their in-depth use in the student's life pattern is far more possible through their memorization, which enables the learning to become a part of his associative thought pattern and, sometimes, a part of his beliefs." I like Robert Frost's comment, "Pretty things that are well said—it's nice to have them in your head."

In the final analysis, you and I are probably most influenced by our personal experiences. I must frankly admit that I did not enjoy learning memory selections. Memorizing was very hard work for me. I found the recitations very boring. I also know that I am handicapped because I did not learn some assignments well enough. I memorized the Old Testament books very well and that has helped me every time I have looked for a passage in the Old Testament. I did not learn the New Testament books as well and so I cannot find certain selections from Paul's letters in the same quick manner. It has been helpful to know the first stanza of many hymns. They can be sung from memory. There are a few key Bible passages which I continue to quote. Many have been forgotten. I would appreciate having learned fewer passages, reviewed them more often, and been required to memorize the exact Bible references for these passages. Referring frequently to a concordance in order to find these references is very time consuming.

I have met many people who despise Christian education because of their unhappy experience with memory work. These persons' distaste for memory work can usually be attributed to one or more of the following reasons:

1. Learning memory selections was very difficult for them.
2. Memory selections were assigned, but there was no

assistance in helping the person learn the selection.
3. Recitation of memory selections was a monotonous, boring routine with little variation.
4. Memory assignments were often long and difficult and many times they appeared to have limited value in the spiritual life and growth of the person.

In spite of the problems associated with memory work and some of my own unpleasant experiences, I consider it an important part of Christian education if the following principles are adhered to:

1. The memory selections should be carefully chosen on the basis of their meaning and value for living the Christian faith and sharing the Christian faith with others.
2. The content should be correlated with the child's moral and spiritual development and should be adapted to individual differences based on the child's ability to memorize.
3. Teaching-learning activities for memorizing should include a maximum of 20% of the total teaching-learning time and usually not involve more than 15 minutes of any period.
4. The teaching-learning process in memorizing should be an enjoyable and meaningful learning experience.
5. Meaningful review and application of the memory selections should be an important part of the curriculum.

1. *Choose Memory Selections with Care*

Memory selections should be those words which will have special meaning and significance throughout life. For most children this will include significant Bible selections, portions of Luther's Small Catechism, and selected stanzas from popular Christian hymns. It is much better to include a limited number of Bible selections, learn the references, and review these selections more often. I would encourage the teaching staff to agree on a basic list of 100 passages to be memorized by the end of grades seven and eight. Other selections could be optional.

Memorizing the first stanzas of 50 hymns and other especially meaningful stanzas should be adequate. This would usually require memorizing less than one new hymn stanza each month.

Meaningful portions of Luther's Catechism should also be memorized. Some of the sections included in the Lord's Prayer, section three of Baptism, and the last four sections of Confession are especially difficult for some children to memorize. I would make those portions of the Catechism an optional assignment. Those children who find it difficult to memorize such selections might be requested to explain the meanings of these selections in their own words. I cannot agree with those who insist that the entire Small Catechism must be memorized. They seem to infer that Luther's explanations are the inspired Word.

2. *Correlate Content with the Child's Development*

Young children can learn memory selections quickly. Much of their learning is accomplished through repetition. There is often a tendency to encourage very young children to memorize selections which have little or no meaning for them. Young children can probably repeat Luther's explanations of the sixth and 10th commandments, but they would have very little meaning for them. Young children perceive concrete ideas rather than abstract concepts. Ronald Goldman's research helps us to understand the thought processes of young children. This can be illustrated with one child's response to the question, "Why didn't Jesus turn the stones into bread?" The child replied, "Because the devil didn't say please." That's a concrete answer. The theologically abstract adult answer would have little meaning for a young child. Memorizing the Holy Communion section of the Catechism several years before the child is allowed to be a participant would be of questionable value. The teachable moment is when the child is preparing to participate in his first Communion. Because many young children can memorize very easily, there may be a tendency to encourage memorizing selections which have little or no meaning for the child. This temptation should be strongly resisted.

Memory selections which serve as a guide in husband-wife or any type of sexual relationships will have little meaning before the junior high years. The rate of forgetting for selections which have little or no meaning for the child is very high. The hope that such selections will be recalled in later life is not based on reliable research.

3. *Keep the Teaching-Learning Period Short*

Although we believe that memorizing Bible selections is an important activity we do not believe that it should receive top priority in teaching the Word. A maximum of 20% of the period should be devoted to memorizing during most sessions. During an average session of 15 minutes for teaching memory selections, I would suggest the following average time allotments.

A. *Five minutes for explanation, reading, and suggested applications of the new selection.*

Be sure that all children can read the selection. Younger children may need help in learning to pronounce all the words. Let several children explain the selection in their own words. Let several chidren comment on possible uses for the passages. Try to share one situation where you have used or plan to use this selection.

B. *Five minutes for learning the new selection.*

Read the selection aloud together. If it is a long passage, repeat the first phrase together and then add the next phrase. At the close of this period, at least one-third of the children should be able to recite the selection. Many teachers do not realize the difficulty of memorizing because they have not memorized any new material recently. You will have a better appreciation if you will also memorize new selections.

C. *Five minutes for recitation and discussion of applications in the following session.*

The recitation of the memory selection takes place in the following session. Actually, it begins the learning period. Ask for volunteers to repeat the selection. More hesitant children and those who are unsure can continue the learning process as they listen to others repeat the selection. Do not provide help with words. The selection is of little value if the child cannot repeat it without assistance. Use positive motivation with comments such as: "You spoke those words with a great deal of expression and feeling." "I like the way you pronounce those words and project your voice." "You spoke that passage with good voice tone." "You said that selection in a pleasant, conversational manner." "You spoke those words in a manner which told me that they are important to you."

It is important not to scold or shame the child who has difficulty memorizing. There are many people who have negative feelings about Christian education, the church, and the Savior because of bad experiences with memorizing. Concentrate on positive statements and positive motivation in most situations.

4. *Make Memorizing an Enjoyable Experience*

When referring to teaching-learning activities, we often discuss Bible reading, music, worship, etc., but we usually refer to memory WORK. We do not refer to reading work, or math work, or music work, but when we refer to the area of memorizing, we frequently list the subject area as work. The immediate connotation is that memorizing is something that is hard, unpleasant, and uninteresting to the child. If we need two words to label the activity of memorizing the Word, I would prefer listing the activity as memory selections.

Memorizing can be made a more enjoyable experience. Keep in mind that learning together is more fun than trying to learn alone. The positive, enthusiastic attitude of the teacher will serve as an excellent model and help motivate learning. In the last section, I briefly described a teaching-learning period. If the same approach were used without variation, it would quickly become the most boring period of the day. The following teaching-learning activities can provide the necessary variety. Use those activities which the children enjoy most and appear to provide the best learning results. Allow children to select the learning activities sometimes. You might also give an individual child an opportunity to select the "game" on or near his birthday.

Many selections can be learned with a minimum amount of effort by including them as part of worship. Luther's explanation of the second article of the Apostles' Creed is especially appropriate as a confesson of faith during the Lenten season. The third article could be used during Pentecost. A systematic use of various Bible, hymn, and catechism selections in worship during appropriate sessions is an excellent way to learn new selections and recall previously memorized materials.

One teacher assisted with the learning of new materials by placing them on newsprint and using them during worship. The visual reminder was also present in this approach. Wall mottoes, posters, and banners can also be used to provide a visual impact. Visual illustrations of the meaning or application of the passage can be very helpful.

The position of the words can assist with learning the meaning and with the memorization of certain selections. I find the second example much easier to remember. It makes a much greater visual impact and is more meaningful for me.

Example 1:

"The Lord is my shepherd, I shall not
want; He makes me lie down in green
pastures."

Example 2:

"The Lord is my shepherd,
    I shall not want;
He makes me lie down
        in green pastures."

Using visual symbols and words can make a visual impact and be an aid to remembering. Symbols might be used for the words in parentheses in the following selection.

"The (Word) is a (lamp) to my (feet) and a (light) to my (path)."

Psalm 119:105

Another approach is to place the selection on the chalkboard. Begin erasing key words and call on various children to recite the passage. Keep erasing key words until all of the words have been erased.

Furnishing each child with a memory notebook in which they copy the assigned passages is helpful. If my wife asks me to pick up three items at the grocery store, I usually have to phone home because I can only remember two of the items. If I write all three items on a slip of paper, I seldom have to refer to the paper because the process of writing has helped me to remember. The memory notebook can be a helpful tool for memorizing and also for reviewing the passages. Let each child design the cover and illustrate the memory selection.

Request that children underline the selections they have memorized in their personal Bible. This process helps the child see the Bible selection in context. It may also help the child remember its approximate location. As the child reads the Bible, there is a visual reminder of the selections memorized if they have been underlined in a distinctive manner or a special color.

One of the biggest mistakes that most children make is to stop learning after they can repeat the selection one time. This practice can be compared to quitting the race about one-third of the distance from the finish line. The rate of forgetting is extremely rapid if the learning process is stopped when the child can repeat the selection once without a mistake. It is at this point that the learning process should concentrate on repeating the selection with good expression, voice tone, and diction. It is during this final third of the learning process that the selection becomes more than a mere repetition of words and becomes an important concept for the child. Overlearning is a very important technique when learning Bible selections.

Larry Richards in his parents' pocket guide entitled, "Helping My Child Memorize Scripture," refers to the first part of the learning process as reciting and the final part as rehearsal. The rehearsal period helps to burn the passage into one's memory, encourages remembering, and slows the process of forgetting. There is a greater possibilty of a particular selection becoming important in the life of the child if the child participates enthusiastically in the rehearsal period.

5. *Provide for Review and Application*

The rapid rate of forgetting is probably the most important reason for questioning the time spent on memory selections. One survey revealed that only 58% of the confirmands, 37% of the high school students, and 22% of the Sunday school teachers could recall portions of Luther's Small Catechism which they had memorized. Limited review of these memory selections is probably the greatest reason for the rapid rate of forgetting. Most of our religion curricula do not provide a systematic review of memory selections. Many pastors have indicated to me that older people seem to remember hymns much better than other memory selections. The reason may be that there are regular opportunities to review the various hymns as they are sung during worship services. Memory selections which are included in the worship service, such as the Lord's Prayer and Apostles' Creed, are usually well-remembered. It is important to provide similar opportunities for reviewing the Bible verses that have been memorized.

Children enjoy games. Many games can be developed which will help reviewing become an enjoyable learning experience. You may wish to adapt the following games to your own needs. They may also provide ideas for developing your own games. It is important to insist on perfect recall in these games; otherwise, there will be too many judgment calls and it will be difficult to be fair to both teams. There is also much better active listening when you insist on perfect recall because the opposing team is listening for any mistake.

I am Thinking of a Bible Verse

Start the game with a statement similar to this: I am thinking of a Bible verse that tells me that the Bible is inspired by God. The first child to state the correct passage *without error* makes the next statement.

Memory Baseball

Divide the group into two teams. Place three empty chairs for first, second, and third base. A correct response is a hit. An incorrect response is an out. The teacher asks for, "A Bible verse that tells me not to curse" or "that tells me to forgive" or "that tells me that God has chosen me as His child." After three successive outs for one team, the next team would get a home run if the "batter" could recall the passage. Insist on perfect recall. A similar game can be developed for basketball.

Memory Cards

Memory selections can be placed on one side of a 3 x 5 card. The reverse side could have an appropriate statement for the verse such as: "A reminder not to covet"; "The First Commandment"; "A hymn stanza which talks about the village where Jesus was born."

Other Activities

Memory selections may also be regularly chosen to be included in the class worship or as a basis for a devotion. A collection of articles, pictures, and applications of specific memory selections could be shared at appropriate times by the teacher. Keep a file of appropriate stories and applications. Every opportunity should be used to coordinate, review, and recall specific memory selections which are appropriate during discussions at other times during the class session. Songs should be sung from memory at appropriate times. Brief review periods during the final minutes or during presession time can be used effectively.

CONCLUSION

If you agree with Robert Frost, then teach memory selections creatively, with joy, enthusiasm, and a senstivity to children's learning abilities and needs. You don't remember what Robert Frost said? Maybe you should memorize his comment.

"Pretty things that are well said—
it's nice to have them in your head."

Chapter 8

How to Evaluate Your Effectiveness As a Teacher

Les Schmidt

TEACHER GOALS

"I don't know if the children learned anything in Sunday school today. It seems like they didn't get very much out of the lesson."

Quite likely you have heard this remark from other teachers in your Sunday school. Possibly you have asked these questions yourself. You and other Sunday school teachers do wonder at times whether or not you got the message of the lesson across to your students.

At such times you may ask yourself how well you are teaching. Did you handle the information correctly? Did you make it interesting? Did you apply the lesson to the students where they are?

To discover the answers to these questions you need to evaluate yourself as a teacher, the materials and techniques you use, and the students. The overall purpose of evaluating is for you to become a better, more effective teacher of the Word of God so the message of God's love in Jesus touches the heart of every student and works changes in their lives.

Know Your Goals

You are critical to the teaching-learning process. How you conduct your Sunday school ministry will greatly influence the degree of effectiveness of your lesson sessions. Therefore, in evaluating your Sunday school ministry you can best begin with yourself. Identify the strong points in your ministry and build on these. Note the weaknesses and seek to improve those areas.

Before you can evaluate, you must first know clearly what it is that you want to measure. For this purpose you need objectives against which to measure your progress.

First, there are general objectives that pertain to your entire Sunday school ministry. What are the goals your congregation seeks to achieve through its Sunday school ministry? In fairness to you and other teachers, the congregation through such responsible groups as its board of Christian education ought to write out specifically what it wants to accomplish through the Sunday school. For example, they may expect each child to be able to participate intelligently in the worship service. Through the Sunday school students are to learn the hymns used in church, to understand the liturgy, to be able to pray the Lord's Prayer and recite the Apostles' Creed from memory, and to behave reverently in church. Or, the congregation may expect Sunday school students by the eighth grade to be able to retell 100 selected Bible narratives, to be able to recite the text of Luther's Small Catechism and 75 selected Bible passages, and to know the books of the Bible. Unconsciously, the congregation has many expectations of its Sunday school. These need to be stated clearly and written down so teachers know what is expected of them. Moreover, the congregation does well to plan a total program in which certain learnings are attached to each grade level. Which Bible passages are to be memorized in the first grade? The second grade? The seventh grade?

As a teacher you have your own objectives you hope to accomplish through your Sunday school teaching. What are they? Write them down so you are clear in your own mind as to what you hope to achieve.

In addition to general objectives that cover your entire Sunday school ministry, each lesson has its own objectives or desired outcomes. These are usually stated in your teachers guide. As you study the lesson and reflect on the students you teach, you may think of other desired outcomes appropriate for, and needed by, the individuals you teach. Write these down in your teachers guide as you prepare your lesson for the next Sunday.

Objectives, the goals you seek to reach, are best stated in terms of changes of behavior you hope to see in students as a result of your ministry. These changes may be in the student's understanding of content, his or her attitudes and feelings, skills, and actions. For example, an attitude objective might be that students may love God's Word and therefore read willingly ten verses from the Bible each day. Ability to use a Bible concordance would be a skill objective.

If objectives are to help you evaluate your effectiveness as a teacher, they must be so stated that progress can be measured. For example, a knowledge objective might be that the student be able to recite in order the names of the books of the New Testament. You can then measure student progress by asking them to recite the names of the New Testament books.

Not only are objectives useful to give direction to your teaching but they also are the basis upon which to evaluate your work. Of course, your students will never meet fully the objectives of the Sunday school, but we hope they continue to make progress toward achievement.

Procedures

Not only do you want to know how well your students are progressing toward the Sunday school and lesson goals, but you also want to know how well your teaching procedures help students attain the goals. For example, if your goal is that students be able to recite the Apostles' Creed, you will not ask them to cut out church symbols—although you may later use this activity to reinforce certain truths expressed in the Creed.

One way to evaluate the effectiveness of your procedures is to observe the students during the lesson session. Do they seem enthusiastic and intent on the lesson? Are their minds wandering? Are they participating in the discussion? Of course, many factors enter into class attitudes. It may be the particular Sunday, or the specific lesson. Recent events in the community or in the student's life can be distracting. In evaluating the effectiveness of your teaching procedures you must also be aware of these factors.

Your effectiveness as a teacher will also be affected by the setting in which you must teach, much of which you can control. Consider these two settings and ask yourself which is more conducive to good learning.

In the first setting the students sit in straight rows of chairs in a room without decorations or pictures on the walls. In this drab, lifeless classroom, the teacher does all the talking; the students simply listen but are given little or no opportunity to respond. After the lecture, the students are asked to fill out blanks in a workbook but are not permitted to ask or discuss any of the questions.

In the second setting the students are seated in a circle so they have eye contact with one another as well as with the teacher. The room is bright and cheerful. The students actively seek out information in small groups. They are encouraged to find the answers on their own; the teacher serves as a guide and resource person. Each student has the opportunity to ask questions, to make comments, and to respond to the teacher and other students. Although the teacher lectures very little, learning is taking place.

Why is the second setting more desirable?

Other elements are important for a setting that will aid the learning process. A proper room temperature, good lighting, cheerful colors, and furniture of a size appropriate for the students are a few of the factors that contribute to a classroom setting conducive for learning. In your evaluation be sure to examine the kind of setting in which you teach and note improvements that might be made.

Variety

Your style as a teacher depends largely on the students you have and on the lessons. However, if you use the same style of teaching for every lesson, you will eventually lose the interest and participation of students. You need variety in your presentations to stimulate and maintain interest. As you evaluate your teaching, note the different styles you use from Sunday to Sunday.

Sensitivity to Students

Your task is not merely to teach the lesson. You are teaching people; the lesson is merely the means to help you teach your students. Therefore, you must know your students and understand their individual backgrounds.

How well do you know your students and how sensitive are you to their needs and interests? Can you describe the hobbies and interests each student in your class has? How well is each person doing in school? How well do you know the parents of each pupil? When were you last in the homes of your students? When was the last time you discussed with a student a personal hurt that that individual was experiencing? Which students are slow learners? Which are gifted? Who can sing? What instruments do the students play? Who finds it extremely difficult to memorize? These are a few questions you might ask yourself as you determine how well you know your students and how sensitive you are to their personalities, needs, and interests.

Am I Prepared?

As you evaluate your teaching, you will also determine how well prepared you were. Was I thoroughly familiar with the lesson material? Was my introduction to the lesson interesting? Did I start at a point familiar to the students and then proceed to the lesson in logical steps? Did I hold the attention of the students? Did I speak clearly and distinctly? Was I enthusiastic about the lesson? Were my questions specific and clear? Did I review the goals and lesson at the end?

What About My Emotions?

The emotions you feel during the session can affect your teaching effectiveness. Even though you may try to hide a "splitting headache," or feelings of hostility toward individual students, you still will likely communicate those feelings to your group. Take an inventory of your feelings towards individual students and try to change negative emotions you may have. By the power of the Spirit seek to be as loving to all students, also the unlovable, as the God who loved us and gave Himself for us who so often ignore or even hate Him.

To set a positive emotional tone for your class, prepare yourself emotionally in advance. Get a good night's sleep so you will be refreshed for the great work of teaching in Sunday school. Arise sufficiently early so you can have a leisurely breakfast and spend some time in your private devotions and in reviewing your lesson preparation before setting out for Sunday school. In your private devotions consider each student and his or her needs and then include those needs in your prayers. Ask God to give you patience, understanding, love, and other blessings of the Spirit.

You As the Lesson

To illustrate another important aspect of teacher evaluation, let me share an incident that actually happened in a church one Sunday morning. The pastor was on vacation and a substitute pastor was taking his place. The guest pastor invited the children to come up for a children's talk. He began his object lesson by asking whether anyone knew him. All the children shook their heads "no." One little three-year-old girl said, "I know the other Jesus!"

We are the vehicle through which children begin to identify with God. In the eyes of some little ones, we even become God. It is important for you as a teacher to take a good look at the attitude you portray to the students you teach. Do your students really know that you are a Christian? Are they aware of the love you have for your Savior? Is there an attitude or a way by which you let students know you have a real love for your Lord? Are you excited about teaching the love of Jesus to your pupils?

It's good for us to look into the mirror to see what kind of image we portray to our students. We should always keep in mind that we are the avenue by which our students begin to know more fully God's love in Jesus Christ. We need to set an example for our students to follow by our own regular church attendance, study of God's Word, and prayer.

STUDENT GOALS

As a Sunday school teacher you must face the fact that your students may come to Sunday school for reasons and motives different from yours. Realizing that they must attend school during the week because they are compelled to do so, some children approach Sunday school with a similar attitude. They attend because they have to go. Moreover, they may regard the Sunday school lesson as an academic subject similar to those in the day school. They are there to get some facts to store mentally, but that is about all. Some may even feel that in Sunday school it is "pass or fail God."

Others may come to Sunday school to meet with friends or because they have nothing else to do. Some may come to avoid a nagging feeling of guilt they would have if they missed Sunday school. You may think of other questionable motives and goals in the minds of your students for their Sunday school attendance.

Your Challenge

Of course, your desire is to cultivate in your students proper motives and reasons for Sunday school participation. Actually, the primary arena in which these motives and attitudes are born and nourished is the home. The strongest motivating force for cultivating in students love for God, His Word, and His church is the Christian family.

However, everything that happens in your classroom will affect the attitudes of students toward God and the church and therefore is a highly significant part of your ministry. Your task is to seek to make the students' learning of Jesus Christ meaningful for them and their lives.

Observation

How can you evaluate the growth of your students in positive attitudes, motives, and goals? One possibility is observing student behavior in class. You can observe the student's "body language." For example, a student can indicate involvement or non-involvement by the way he or she sits. Picture, if you will, a student sitting at his desk, slouched down, eyes on the ceiling, apparently daydreaming. Picture next to him a student who is sitting straight, attentively looking at the teacher, eyes bright, apparently absorbed in the lesson. These two simple examples will indicate which student is involved and which is not.

"Body language" can be deceptive, however. It may be that the slouching, non-attentive student always behaves that way. And the apparently attentive student may actually be absorbed in creating a good impression. Should you question these two students, it may be that the first student will answer readily and accurately; the "attentive" student may not. Nevertheless, "body language" can help you evaluate student involvement if observed cautiously.

Listening

Student goals and attitudes can be noted by their verbal responses. You may begin a session, "Today, girls and boys, we are going to hear about Cain and Abel." You may get the immediate response, "Aw, we heard that story before." The students already have evaluated the lesson before you have hardly begun. But they also have alerted you to the fact that if you are to be effective this Sunday, you must make a quick adjustment and present the narrative in a way that is fresh and exciting for your students.

Through the wise use of questions you can gain new insights into the attitudes of your students. For example, in the narrative of the widow's mite, you might ask students what they think of a person giving all she has to God. Follow-up questions may reveal the degree of responsibility your students feel toward God for all aspects of their lives. With older youth you can ask such discussion-provoking questions as, "Do you think paying taxes is giving to God?" Through responses to such questions you can learn what students think and value and be able to guide them to a better understanding of the Christian faith and its meaning for their lives.

You can learn to know the motives, attitudes, values, and goals of your students better also through friendly conversation. For your conversation to be friendly it is important that you show respect for the thoughts of your students even though you may disagree, be courteous in your responses, and honor the student as an individual person. Through conversation you will get cues for your task as a guide for the learning of the students, and perhaps informally teach—even though you may not realize that you are teaching.

Another way to learn to know students better is to ask students to apply lesson truths to real life situations. You might ask, "What would you do if . . . ?" This gives the student opportunities to apply the lesson thought to situations that affect him. You will discover whether the student has grasped the point of the lesson, and the student will see the effect the lesson is to have on his or her life.

You know what you want to see happen in Sunday school, but you need to learn what students expect. A few techniques for accomplishing this have been described; in your genuine concern for your students you will think of other ways.

EVALUATION DEVICES

There are numerous ways and devices you can use to evaluate the effectiveness of your lesson presentation on a given Sunday. Some of these involve the participation of the students. However, some of the student evaluations can be threatening and not particularly helpful or even accurate.

The time-honored "review" is a helpful device not only for ascertaining how much the students learned but also for reinforcing the lesson in the students' minds. At the conclusion of a session you might ask students to review for you what they have learned. At the beginning of the session on the following Sunday you might ask them to summarize what they had learned the week before. The second review will also inform you how well the students retained the previous week's learning. Reviews that students write can be even more helpful in that students will reinforce their learnings through the process of writing them on paper. Oral review has the advantage that you can correct immediately any mislearnings the students may have.

Another form of review is the asking of specific questions on points of the lesson. Be sure to include thought or application questions in addition to those that call for recall of factual details. You may wish to add such questions as: Did the introduction to the lesson attract their attention? Did they feel involved in the discussion? Did they find the story interesting? What parallels from the story did they find for their own lives? In asking questions such as these, be sure that the students evaluate the story and its presentation, but not you as a person.

The use of an imaginary line is another device that can be used. This line would be a continuum from totally interested to totally disinterested. The question might be: How interesting for your life today did you find this story? Then students would position themselves on this imaginary line according to their reception of the lesson. Actually, through this device the student rather than the teacher is being evaluated. It may be interesting to discover why a student may have found a particular lesson to be uninteresting.

If you use the imaginary line technique, you will want to ask a few "warm-up" questions about the students' interest in various aspects of their life in school and community. If you focus completely on the lesson presentation, you may inadvertently lead students to believe that they can stand in judgment on the Word of God itself. Actually, you are seeking to evaluate student interests, and, through this technique, you can ascertain what those interests are and how you might better present the lesson in ways that will capture that interest.

Another device to use in evaluating ways to present the lesson more effectively is to ask students to rank various methods of presentation from 10 to one in order of attractiveness. Through this device you can get clues as to how best to conduct your class sessions. However, the most popular method may not be the best to use. What you seek to accomplish through a certain learning activity will determine the method you use.

One instrument you might construct to help you evaluate your teaching is the checklist. In your preparation for the Sunday's lesson, prepare a list of questions that cover everything you wish to accomplish in the session. After the presentation, go over the checklist to ascertain how well you achieved your goals.

You might invite a teacher whom you trust to visit your class to observe the teaching-learning process that occurs during the Sunday school session. The observer later can review the class session with you to identify things that worked well and to point out ways in which the teaching might be improved.

The tape recorder can be used for self-evaluation. Tape the Sunday morning session. Later at home, replay the tape to analyze the lesson presentation and class reaction. During your first replaying of the tape you might focus on your part in the session and identify the strengths and weaknesses in the presentation. Then, you might play the tape the second time to evaluate the quality of student interaction. With a list of students before you, check each name as that person asks a question or contributes to the discussion. You may discover that some students dominate the session, while others contribute little or nothing. You then will seek to focus your attention more on those students who are not active in their participation.

Some congregations have videotape machines. This instrument is an excellent tool to use for self-evaluation. Not only will you be able to hear what was said; you also can see what happened during the session. You perhaps will note some distracting mannerisms you have which you would like to eliminate.

These are a few of the possibilities you have for evaluation. Always remember, however, that the purpose of evaluation is not to determine your worth either as a person or as a teacher. Through evaluation you will be able to identify areas that need improvement and thus be able to become more effective in your important ministry. Likewise, student evaluation is not to measure student worth, but to help you identify areas in which individual students need help and thus to equip you to be a better minister of Jesus Christ to those persons.

RESOURCES FOR IMPROVEMENT

Without the stimulation of comparing notes and experiences with other Sunday school teachers, you can easily get in a rut. As you hear and see what other teachers are doing, you have a basis for evaluating your work and an opportunity to gain new insights and skills.

The most natural place for evaluation and growth through interaction with other teachers is your own congregational Sunday school teachers meeting. Your staff should meet weekly, or as frequently and regularly as possible, to plan the entire session for each Sunday as well as prepare for each lesson. Many Sunday schools are hurting because the sessions are poorly planned and teachers are ill-prepared.

Another way to check your work and to gain new ideas is to visit other Sunday school classes occasionally. You might visit other classes in your own church, or visit a

Sunday school in your area that has an outstanding Sunday school program.

In many areas of the church Sunday school associations meet regularly, usually twice each year, at which teachers from a cluster of congregations get together for a teacher training program and to compare ideas and experiences. Beyond that, District and churchwide Sunday school conventions and conferences are offered to help teachers grow. In such gatherings you will be reminded of the importance of your ministry as a Sunday school teacher and will get many new ideas to improve your class sessions.

Conversations with your students and their parents will give you new insights into the people you teach and will help you as you teach to meet your students where they are. Through such conversations and home visits, you will discover where you are missing the mark, and find cues for improvement.

A regular program of reading will also help you. You will want to read the Bible and church books regularly to grow in your understanding of the Christian faith you teach. You will also benefit from reading books and magazines that will help you develop better teaching skills and give you a better understanding of people. One excellent periodical just for Sunday school teachers is *Interaction* (Concordia Publishing House, 3558 South Jefferson Avenue, Saint Louis, MO 63118). A Sunday school that provides every teacher with a subscription to a magazine such as *Interaction* makes a wise investment in its Sunday school.

CONCLUSION

One of my favorite Bible passages is Philippians 3:12: "Not that I have already obtained this or am already perfect; but I press on to make it my own, because Christ Jesus has made me His own." This observation is also true of our Sunday school teaching. We will never be perfect, but we can continue to evaluate our ministry and seek to do better. It is this attitude that marks the desirable Sunday school teacher.